Between Fixity and Flux

A Study of the Concept of Poetry in the Criticism of T. S. Eliot

BY

SISTER MARY CLEOPHAS COSTELLO

OF THE

RELIGIOUS SISTERS OF MERCY OF THE UNION

THE CATHOLIC UNIVERSITY OF AMERICA PRESS, INC.
WASHINGTON, D. C. 20017

TABLE OF CONTENTS

PREFACE

Anyone interested in modern criticism can hardly escape the influence of T. S. Eliot. His provocative comments have so pervaded contemporary critical theory that they force one to choose one of two positions: either one must accept his dicta completely; or in refuting his theory, one must examine all critical premises in order to formulate another. The following study is the culmination of many years' attention to Eliot's writings, sharpened three years ago when I began serious work in literary criticism under the direction of Dr. J. C. La Drière of the Catholic University, at whose suggestion I undertook this study.

At his instigation also I visited the Houghton Library of Harvard University to examine the Henry Ware Eliot collection and to gather materials from the unpublished Clark Lectures. Unfortunately, permission to quote from these lectures was not granted. Mr. Eliot's reason for refusing is summed up as follows: "These lectures were written twenty years ago and naturally I do not now agree with everything I said and still less agree with the way in which I said it." It is very difficult to understand the first part of this statement, since one of the conclusions of this essay is that Eliot has been surprisingly consistent in his theoretical position not only during twenty but even during thirty years of critical writing. I am at a loss to know with what he does not agree. Although anything that might have been quoted from these lectures can be paralleled in other portions of his work, in several instances Eliot has stated his thought more clearly in this manuscript than elsewhere, and it is a great loss that this material may not be used for corroborative purposes.

One virtue of a preface is that it offers an opportunity to acknowledge debts of gratitude which accumulate along the road of research. Not only is it a pleasure to recognize these, but I also hope that my measure of grateful appreciation is proportioned to the generosity with which these services were rendered to me. My grateful thanks must go first to my Superiors and Community, who have given me these years at the University and made it possible for me to work under such ideal circumstances. Next I wish to express my gratitude to the faculty of the English Department for sharing their broad scholarship and for being so kindly in their encouragement during my student days, especially to Professors La Drière, Giovannini (who gave his books, too!), and Litz.

To the staff members of the Library of Congress I express sincere thanks for cheerful, efficient service. I owe a note of appreciation to Professor William A. Jackson and Miss Carolyn E. Jakeman for courtesies which were shown to me at the Houghton Library, and to the library officials of Harvard University for allowing me to use the Henry Ware Eliot Catalogue and Collection of the works of T. S. Eliot. My thanks are also due to the following publishers who have allowed me to quote from Eliot's works: Brentano, Inc. for *Anabase;* Faber & Faber for *The Use of Poetry and the Use of Criticism, Selected Essays, What Is a Classic?, After Strange Gods,* and *Essays, Ancient & Modern;* the Harvard University Press for *A Garland for John Donne, 1631-1931;* the Oxford University Press for *Tradition and Experiment, English Critical Essays of the Twentieth Century, The Classics and the Man of Letters, The Wheel of Fire, Studies in Honor of Sir H. J. C. Grierson;* Charles Scribner's Sons for *From Anne to Victoria;* A. A. Knopf for *Ezra Pound, His Metric and Poetry;* Methuen & Co., Ltd. for *The Sacred Wood;* and Jackson, Son & Co. for *The Music of Poetry.*

Sister Mary Cleophas, R.S.M.
Mount Saint Agnes College
Baltimore, Maryland

Feast of St. Michael, 1946

CHAPTER I

TRADITION AND THE INDIVIDUAL CRITIC

The justification for this study has been provided by T. S. Eliot himself. In 1929 when he published his essay, "Experiment in Criticism," he wrote:

> Now, there is an urgent need for experiment in criticism of a new kind, which will consist largely in a logical and dialetical study of the terms used. My own interest in these problems has been fostered partly by dissatisfaction with the *meaning* of my own statements in criticism, and partly by dissatisfaction with the terminology of the Humanists. In literary criticism we are constantly using terms which we cannot define, and defining others by them. We are constantly using terms which have an *inten*sion and an *ex*tension, which do not quite fit; theoretically they ought to be made to fit; but if they cannot, then some other way must be found of dealing with them so that we may know at every moment what we mean.[1]

The purpose of this essay, suggested by Eliot's remarks, is to make a dialectical study of his criticism to determine as far as possible what he means by the word *poetry*. It will, then, be a study in literary theory.

As for systematic study of Eliot's ideas up to the present time, John Hayward's edition of Eliot's criticism, *Points of View*,[2] has, in R. A. Hodgson's words, "the advantage of enabling us to compare his treatment of his chosen themes with that of other writers,"[3]

---

[1] *Tradition and Experiment in Present-Day Literature* (N. Y.: Oxford University Press, 1929), p. 213. Cf. Remy de Gourmont's statement in *Le Problème du Style* (Paris: Mercure de France, 1924), p. 144: "La critique littéraire, qui devrait savoir tout, usera certainement, un jour prochain, de la méthode scientifique dans l'appréciation des oeuvres et des écrivains; jusqu'ici elle se tapit derrière une prudente et forte ignorance."

[2] London: Faber & Faber, 1941.

[3] "Tradition and Mr. Eliot," *The New English Weekly,* XIX (Sept. 25, 1941), 221.

1

but there is no attempt to utilize this material in any other way than as a presentation of well-known texts grouped together under such general titles as "Literary Criticism," "Dramatic Criticism," and "Individual Authors." Mr. Hodgson draws an acute conclusion from this arrangement, however. After observing that it makes it difficult to trace the development of Eliot's thoughts, he continues: "Perhaps this matters less with Mr. Eliot than it would in other cases for, judging by the dates given for the various passages in this book, there has been remarkably little change in his position since 1917."

Hans Häusermann, whose essay carries the promising title, "T. S. Eliot's Conception of Poetry," though admitting that Eliot's theory is by no means revolutionary, declines to synthesize it but prefers to "reconstruct his [Eliot's] concept of poetry from an analysis of his own practice and his achievement as a poet."[4]

Eliot's criticism has been little used for purposes of a theoretical nature but has been applied largely by commentators to the elucidation of his poetry. That is the importance of F. O. Matthiessen's invaluable book.[5] It is likewise the purpose of nine-tenths of the items listed on Eliot in Robert Stallman's "Selective Bibliography on the Criticism of Poetry, 1920-1942" which appeared in *The University Review*.[6] In the commentary of these writers distinctions between literary theory (or "the formulation, objectively and without regard for problems of value, of general knowledge of the nature of literature"), literary criticism (or "the evaluation and in this sense the interpretation of works of literature"), and

---

[4] *Etude de Lettres,* Bulletin de la société des Etudes de Lettres (Oct. 1, 1942, No. 51), p. 166. Herr Häusermann, however, has not confined his observations exclusively to Eliot's method of writing poetry but has drawn his conclusion that Eliot uses poetry to convey his religious convictions from a psychological analysis of the meanings of his poems. Cf. also the same author's "T. S. Eliots Religiöse Entwicklung," *Englische Studien,* LXIX (1935): 372-91. Häusermann also published in 1939 *Studien zur englischen Literaturkritik, 1910-1930.* I have not seen this.

[5] F. O. Matthiessen, *The Achievement of T. S. Eliot* (N. Y.: Oxford University Press, 1935). But for penetrating and judicious application of Eliot's principles, see the same author's *American Renaissance* (N. Y.: Oxford University Press, 1941).

[6] University of Kansas City, X (Autumn, 1943), 65-71.

a theory of criticism (or "the formulation of general principles on the basis of which critical evaluation may be made") have not been too nicely observed.[7] Nor has Eliot observed these distinctions as clearly as he might. But he has written that the critic "who remains worth reading" has asked, if he has only imperfectly answered, "what is poetry?" as well as "is this a good poem?"[8] That Eliot is a critic who remains worth reading can be substantiated by the bibliography cited above.

The following quotation seems to point to the fact that Eliot interprets theory of criticism as literary criticism vitalized by traditional literary theory. Speaking of "traditional criticism" in the essay quoted at the beginning of this chapter, he said that it may mean "following the state of mind of the preceding generation," or "it may be a criticism which has a definite theory of the meaning and value of the term 'tradition,' " and which may be experimental "in reverting to masters who have been forgotten."[9] Since this study purports to be one in literary theory, a concentration on any term would demand not only a study of Eliot's critical writings but an awareness also of those "masters who have been forgotten." At first blush these sources, though apparently as numerous for Eliot's theory as for his poetry, could scarcely be called forgotten. He has acknowledged his indebtedness to Remy de Gourmont in *The Sacred Wood*,[10] and Ants Oras has studied his relationship to Irving Babbitt, Charles Maurras, and Santayana.[11] Matthiessen pointed out that Ezra Pound's influence was one to be reckoned with. "Any detailed study of Eliot's background and development would find a fertile field in determining

---

[7] T. C. Pollock, *The Nature of Literature* (Princeton: Princeton University Press, 1942), pp. xviii-xix.

[8] *The Use of Poetry and the Use of Criticism* (London: Faber & Faber, 1933), p. 16.

[9] *Tradition and Experiment*, p. 198.

[10] Garnet Rees in a short essay, "French Influence on T. S. Eliot," *Revue de Littérature Comparée,* XVI (Oct. 1936), 764-67, calls for a study among French students of Remy de Gourmont's thought, holding that only American critics have utilized his ideas.

[11] *The Critical Ideas of T. S. Eliot* (Tartu: University of Estonia, 1932). It is said that Eliot has commended this study.

how many of his tastes and opinions first crystallized as a result
of his early close association with the author of 'Personae.' "[12]
Matthiessen has also emphasized, despite their "sharp divergence
of approach," Eliot's "kinship to Matthew Arnold." While there
are, doubtless, a few principles which they have in common, Eliot's
perceptions are so much more profound than Arnold's that much
detailed comparison would not be profitable.[13]

But there are other critics to be reckoned with, notably, Coleridge, Dryden, and Aristotle whom Eliot mentioned in *The Sacred
Wood*.[14] The whole purpose of "The Perfect Critic" is to show
that he is seeking for a mind that can be so intellectually honest
and detached that its evaluations are based, as far as it is humanly
possible for them to be, upon intellectual rather than emotional
responses; in short, a mind in which the emotional drive for truth
is so great that the object which is being evaluated is considered
in relation to itself rather than in relation to a subjective reaction.
Such a mind Eliot holds is free. Though Coleridge and Dryden
rank high in Eliot's estimation in the roll-call of critics, neither is
quite the perfect critic for whom he is looking.[15]

---

[12] Matthiessen, *Achievement, op. cit.*, p. 72. Mario Praz has also commented
upon this relationship in "T. S. Eliot and Dante," *Southern Review*, II
(1937) : 525-48. Therefore, Yvor Winters' melodramatic *dénouement* at the
conclusion of the two chapters which he devotes to Eliot in *The Anatomy of
Nonsense* (Norfolk, Conn.: New Directions, 1943) appears a trifle non-
sensical. For criticism of Winters, see *American Bookman*, I (Fall, 1944),
114-115, and T. Weiss, "The Nonsense of Winters' Anatomy," *Quarterly
Review of Literature*, I (Summer, 1944), 300-318.

[13] For a criticism of Eliot's attitude toward Arnold, see M. L. S. Loring,
"T. S. Eliot on Matthew Arnold," *Sewanee Review*, XLIII (October, 1935) :
479-88. Allen Tate has followed Eliot's evaluation of Arnold in "Literature as
Knowledge," *Reason in Madness* (N. Y.: G. P. Putnam's Sons, 1941), pp.
20-61.

[14] *The Sacred Wood* (London: Methuen & Co., 1934, 3rd ed.), pp. 1-16.

[15] J. Isaacs in "Coleridge's Critical Terminology," *Essays and Studies*, XXI
(1936), p. 86 notes the frequency with which the names of Dryden and
Coleridge emerge in a discussion of critical terminology. For a criticism of
Eliot's championship of Dryden, however, see Ezra Pound, *Polite Essays*
(Norfolk, Conn.: New Directions, n. d.), pp. 135-52, and "Mr. Eliot's Mare's
Nest," *The New English Weekly* (March 8, 1934), Pound's review of *The
Use of Poetry* and *After Strange Gods*.

When Eliot turns to the consideration of Aristotle his admiration is unbounded. For Eliot, Aristotle had

> what is called the scientific mind—a mind which as it is rarely found in scientists except in fragments, might better be called the intelligent mind. For there is no other intelligence than this, and so far as artists and men of letters are intelligent . . . their intelligence is of this kind.[16]

The living force of Aristotle is not in accepting him canonically but in observing his "universal" intelligence operating. That is why his "broken treatise" of the *Poetics* may be useful in providing an example "not of laws, or even of method . . . but of intelligence itself swiftly operating the analysis of sensation to the point of principle and definition."[17] It would seem then that Aristotle, as one of the "masters who had been forgotten," would be worthy of attention in clarifying any formulation of a concept of poetry which Eliot might have.

Several difficulties present themselves in pursuing the topic of the present essay. Interested as Eliot has been in the criticism of the twentieth century and valuable as his contribution to it has been, he never re-reads his prose[18] and he has never looked upon himself as a critic but as a poet practicing criticism.[19] Much of

---

[16] *Sac. Wood*, p. 13.

[17] *Ibid.*, p. 11. Not only was Eliot at the time of writing this associating with Ezra Pound, who had said in *The Spirit of Romance* (N. Y.: E. P. Dutton & Sons, n. d.), p. 3: "The triumph of literary criticism is that certain of its terms—chiefly those defined by Aristotle—still retain some shreds of meaning"; but, aside from the philosophical training he had received at Harvard, Eliot read Greek philosophy during the winter of 1915 at Merton College, Oxford. The fruit of this study appeared in "The Development of Leibniz's Monadism" (*Monist,* Oct. 1916), where he made a detailed comparison of the Leibnizian system with Aristotelian hylomorphism.

[18] See *The Music of Poetry* (Glasgow: Jackson Son & Co., 1942), p. 8.

[19] *Sac. Wood,* p. 46: "The creative artist in England finds himself compelled, or at least tempted, to spend much of his time and energy in criticism that he might reserve for the perfecting of his proper work: simply because there is no one else to do it." Mr. Hugh Gordon Porteus' comment upon this is that outside of the artist "there is no single critic of the first order . . .; and very few at all who are not slaves of the general ideas of the time." *Wyndham Lewis* (London: Desmond Harmsworth, 1932), p. 263.

his theory has been confined to the ephemeral form of the periodical essay. Yet the entire body of his critical writings exhibits a remarkable consistency and his theory shows formulation according to a persistent general pattern. But again and again Eliot has refused to reveal in his own work a *differentia* which might integrate his poetic and focus it so that a definition might be formulated for "all poetry." One of the reasons for this refusal is that any "extreme of theorizing about the nature of poetry" is the province of the aesthetician. Such work, he declares, is beyond his limited capacity.[20] Again his excuse seems to beg the question.[21]

If any one writing today realizes that few readers know what poetry is, that person is Eliot. On the other hand, because his taste is so catholic, he recognizes the "poeticity" of many "kinds" which are not covered by ordinary definitions. His criticism, as a matter of fact, has largely been an exposition of why some works should be denominated poetry in the twentieth century, in spite of what former generations have thought of them. But when an examination of his theory is made for the basis of this classification, a curious elusiveness befogs the issue. "Our valuation of poetry," he wrote in the essay on John Dryden, "depends upon several considerations, upon the permanent and upon the mutable and transitory. When we try to isolate the essentially poetic, we bring our pursuit in the end to something insignificant; our standards vary with every poet whom we consider."[22] Works whose standards depend upon the mutable and transitory would indeed be hard to classify according to excellence in any case. "If we only knew

---

[20] *Use of Poetry*, pp. 149-150. In this attitude Eliot may have been influenced by Ezra Pound who wrote in 1917: "Poetry is a composition of words set to music. Most other definitions of it are indefensible, or worse, metaphysical." "Vers Libre and Arnold Dolmetsch," *The Egoist*, IV (1917), 90.

[21] See, *Use of Poetry*, p. 155: "I have not attempted any definition of poetry, because I can think of none which does not falsify by leaving out much more than it can include."

[22] *Selected Essays* (London: Faber & Faber, 1932), pp. 308-309. Cf. the "Introduction" by Eliot to G. Wilson Knight, *The Wheel of Fire* (London: Oxford University Press, 1930), p. xiii: "When I say 'great poetry' I do not suggest that there is a pure element in poetry, the right use of words and cadences, which the real amateur of poetry can wholly isolate to enjoy."

'perfect' poetry," Eliot wrote in 1928, "we should know very little about poetry; we cannot say even who are the twelve, or the six, or the three, or the two 'greatest' poets. But if we really love poetry, then we know and must know all its degrees."[23]

It is just this matter of "degrees" which prevents definition, according to Eliot; for, he maintains, what no definition gives is "an absolute dividing line between Poetry and Not-Poetry." His longest explanation on this subject is given in the following apologia:

> Repeated meditations led me first to suspect, that there are surprisingly few things that can be said about Poetry; and of these few, the most turn out either to be false or to say nothing of significance. There are a great many things worth saying about one kind of poetry or another; and a good many might not have been said if their authors had not been under the impression that they were talking about all Poetry, when they were only talking about the kind of poetry they liked. Those who indulge in the Essence of Poetry fantasy are given to using "touchstones," or test lines, which are almost always true poetry, and usually very great poetry. What none of them gives us, is an absolute dividing line between Poetry and Not-Poetry.[24]

From this, one can see that Eliot's refusal to define is based upon the fact that "when we generalise about poetry . . . we are generalising from the poetry which we best know and best like; not from all poetry, or even all of the poetry which we have read."[25]

---

[23] Ezra Pound, *Selected Poems,* ed. with "Introduction" by T. S. Eliot (London: Faber & Gwyer, 1928), p. xxii. Seeking and explicating the "essentially poetic" presents certain dangers to Eliot. One of these is the fear that lazy people will grasp such a formula to "help them to recognize the best poetry without having to depend upon their own sensibility and taste." *Use of Poetry,* p. 146. Another is that some persons will expect "from poetry some illusory pure enjoyment, of separating poetry from everything else in the world, and cheating themselves out of a great deal that poetry has to give to [their] development." *Ibid.,* p. 116. But Eliot's readers are not exposed to these dangers since "criticism never does find out what poetry is in the sense of arriving at an adequate definition." *Ibid.,* p. 16.

[24] Review of A. E. Housman's *The Name and Nature of Poetry, The Criterion,* XIII (193-34), 153.

[25] *Use of Poetry,* p. 139. See also, p. 109 and p. 141.

Since no one can know "all poetry" or could adequately appreciate it if it were known, Eliot holds that any definition that is formulated must be based upon the individual critic's bias and so does not possess sufficient universality to warrant philosophical consideration.

Whether a satisfactory definition can be synthesized under these circumstances is a challenge. "The true generalization," Eliot wrote in *The Sacred Wood,*

> is not something superimposed upon an accumulation of perceptions; the perceptions do not, in a really appreciative mind, accumulate as a mass, but form themselves as a structure; and criticism is the statement in language of this structure.[26]

In applying this principle to theory David Daiches has cryptically put it thus: "Definition of terms is not a simple matter; it is not the beginning of a thought-process but the end."[27] The direct statements in apparently definitive form which Eliot has made on poetry cannot be considered too seriously as definitions. One— "poetry is a superior amusement"—aside from being a direct quotation from Remy de Gourmont,[28] is a definition in terms not of genus and *differentia,* but of *officium* or end, and involves a contradiction of Eliot's own dictum that "poetry is . . . not to be defined by its uses."[29]

Poetry in its matter is related to all other forms of discourse because it employs speech. Therefore, the subject of this investigation is to determine from Eliot's statements the form of speech which he thinks poetry takes so as to differentiate it from all other forms of discourse. The great diversity of opinion which exists in modern criticism arises largely from confusion in the minds of critics about the fundamental issues of their science. Some of this diversity is due to lack of historical perspective, some to erroneous application of modern psychological theories,

---

[26] *Sac. Wood,* p. 15.

[27] *New Literary Values* (London: Oliver and Boyd, 1936), p. 9.

[28] This has been noted by Oscar Cargill, *Intellectual America* (N. Y.: Macmillan Co., 1941), p. 273.

[29] *Use of Poetry,* p. 155.

and some to impatience with theory for its own sake. Today Mr. Richards wishes to substitute the emotions derived from poetry for the knowledge and practice of religion.[30] Croce mistakes the beginning of the artistic process for the end.[31] Mr. Ransom is seeking an esoteric ontological knowledge from poetry.[32] Mr. Kazin lauds Edmund Wilson because he examines literature to "make life practicable."[33] It is obvious that these critics are talking at cross purposes because they are not agreed upon the nature of what they are talking about. It is by studying the nature of a thing that we learn most easily what it is for.

That Eliot is just as aware as any one how basic this question of the nature of poetry is can be shown by the fact that in *The Sacred Wood* he remarked casually that there have been two great theories regarding poetry: the Aristotelian and the Horatian.[34] And, he added, it is the latter which has had the greater influence. But by one of those elusive evasions, propped up by plausible excuses, which at times characterize his work, he has refused to commit himself as to his own affiliations on this question of the nature of poetry, or at least he has avoided any direct statement upon it.

Bertram Higgins has remarked upon this unsatisfactoriness of Eliot's in what he calls his "general criticism," or what I prefer to call his theory. Asserting that Eliot's method in "particular criticism" is apt and penetrating, Mr. Higgins defines his methods as "a device of securing utter clarity to the argument by eliminating from it those issues . . . which, for reasons apparent in the context, are insusceptible of equally definitive treatment."[35] How-

---

[30] I. A. Richards, *Principles of Literary Criticism* (2d ed.; N. Y.: Harcourt, Brace & Co., 1926), pp. 44-57.

[31] *Aesthetics,* tr. Douglas Ainslie (London: Macmillan & Co., 1922).

[32] John Crowe Ransom, *The New Criticism* (Norfolk, Conn.: New Directions, 1941), pp. 332-336.

[33] A. Kazin, *On Native Grounds* (N. Y.: Reynal & Hitchcock, 1942), p. 452.

[34] *Sac. Wood,* p. 11.

[35] "The Critical Method of T. S. Eliot," *Scrutinies,* II, ed. E. Rickword (London: Wishart & Co., 1931), p. 67.

ever, if this method, Higgins holds, is applied to theory the losses are greater than the gains, for

> a general subject is not an actualised coherence, but a radiating center of possibilities which are directed and bounded by the "terms of reference" in its nomenclature. Therefore to follow up one essential line of inquiry in such a subject and entirely to shun another is to benefit a part and not the whole, for the part tends to become a subject independent of it.[36]

The justness of this observation, however, is rightly chargeable not only to Eliot but to every other practicing critic. That is why, seeing the necessity for it, Eliot called in 1929 for a "logical and dialectical study of the terms used" in literary criticism. To define terms is the work of the philosopher and the aesthetician: but the literary critic must furnish them with the data for generalization. Moreover, as Eliot pointed out in "Experiment in Criticism," though the literary critic must never overstep the bounds of his science, he must be aware of what is happening on the frontiers of the numerous other fields which border upon his. In Eliot's work one extenuation may be made; when he ignores a subject, he is at least aware that he *is* ignoring it. The *differentia* of poetry is one such lacuna in his literary theory. It is the modest purpose of this study to try to derive a synthetic description of this one concept from the numerous pronouncements relevant to it which Eliot has made.

Because this essay purports to be a "dialectical study," I have quoted at length from Eliot's criticism passages which have been used so frequently that they have begun "to lose their savour." This, though pedantic, I have done for scientific accuracy. I do not hope to explicate anything new or startling but only to mark certain directions in his thought. One finds after reading the mass of commentary that has been written about Eliot that the pet intuitions which flash upon one's mind as original insights, have all flashed with deeper significance upon some one else earlier (or at least, they have been printed sooner). This evidence of interest is gratifying because the roll-call of his critics shows that the finest

---

[36] *Ibid.,* pp. 67-68.

literary minds of our generation have grappled with his thought. It is fitting too that the obvious but less spectacular deductions should be left for the student.

The principle upon which this investigation is based is an examination of the formal cause which Eliot attributes to poetry. In the Aristotelian scheme of causality there are four causes which account fully for the mode of being of a thing; two of these, the efficient and final causes, are extrinsic to the object; the material and formal causes are intrinsic to the object. That by which an effect is produced is the efficient cause. If a thing exists and if existence does not belong to it as a constituent of its own self, then the fact of its existence presupposes that it has received its existence from something else. What effects this change is the agent or efficient cause. In the making of poetry, the poet is the efficient cause, but it is well always to remember that the efficiency of his action affects not the poet but the thing made.

The final cause of poetry determines the reason for the poet's trying to fashion speech in just this way which has been called poetry. If poetry is conceded to be an art, then here, if anywhere, teleological design should be apparent. However one may think of nature, art does not just "occur." In one sense, of course, one may say that the final cause is intrinsic in an object in so far as the nature of that object will determine its use; one cannot do with a Gothic cathedral, for example, what one can do with a symphony. But in considering the final cause one must distinguish between the end as attained and the end as intended. "It is not the end as attained that is the final cause; as attained it is an effect pure and simple. It is the end as intended that is a final cause; and as intended it does not yet actually exist."[37] As intended, the final cause has no physical reality; it is an attraction which operates upon the efficient agent to prompt him to action.

These two extrinsic causes will be mentioned incidentally in the course of the discussion of this paper as their notice contributes to a clarification of the main thesis of the two "intrinsic" causes. The material cause is that out of which a thing is made. "Words," said Eliot in 1917, "are perhaps the hardest of all

---

[37] Peter Coffey, *Ontology* (N. Y.: Peter Smith, 1938), p. 412.

material of art."[38] But while words are the matter for the poet, words in themselves as the poet uses them, are not just pure matter; *that* is sound. By combining letters sound structures are formed; by attaching conventional significations to these, meaning structures are erected. Both of these in turn unite to form syntactic and grammatical constructions. Therefore, what writers use is never pure matter as such, but matter which has had many formal elements imposed upon it. Furthermore, it is not "language" in the abstract, as it were, which the poet uses, but, according to Eliot, "one's language as it is spoken at one's own time."[39] This is the material of poetry.

The formal cause, or form, is "that which makes a thing what it is." Since we are seeking to know how Eliot differentiates poetry from everything else, the form becomes the crucial area for investigation. This cause is the principle which gives shape or character or structure to a work. But it is not structure in the narrow sense of that term, that is, the skeletal pattern upon which the work is built, but "all that determines specific character." Meaning especially, then (which too often is referred to as non-formal "content," "substance," etc.), is a formal element. For the Aristotelian, accordingly, a work of art contains not only one but many formal elements, the sum total of which is *the* form. As Professor La Drière explains it,

> this total form will extend ideally throughout the work; the work will be all meaning, all structure. But it [the work] will equally be all that which is given meaning, that which has structure. . . . Where there is form there will be matter, informed; where there is matter there will be form, informing. To separate the matter and the form of the work will require a mental abstraction; in the actual thing the two will be a unity, since it is only by their union that the thing exists.[40]

---

[38] *Ezra Pound, His Metric and Poetry* (N. Y.: A. Knopf, 1917), p. 14.

[39] "That Poetry Is Made with Words," *The New English Weekly,* XV (Apr. 27, 1939), 28.

[40] J. C. La Drière, Shipley's *Dictionary,* art. "Form," p. 250. Further explanation of the causes may be obtained from the following: Aristotle, *Physics,* ii, 3; *Metaphysics,* i, 3; and v, 2. R. P. Phillips, *Modern Thomistic Philoso-*

Of these formal elements those which are significant for the present purpose are structure of sound, meanings, and structure of meaning. Differences in structure of sound provide for the classification of all literature into *prose* and *verse,* according to the more or less high patterning of the phonetic structure of the work. Reference to the meanings afford a formal element whereby a work may be classified according to *genre.* And the differences in the general literary forms, expository, narrative, and dramatic, provide for differentiation on the basis of structure of meaning.[41] Relevant passages in Eliot's criticism have been grouped and discussed on this basis. The first of these—structure of sound—will be treated in the next chapter.

------

phy (London: Burns, Oates, & Washbourne, 1934), II, Chap. IX. Cardinal Mercier, *A Manual of Modern Scholastic Philosophy,* tr. by T. L. and S. A. Parker (London: Kegan Paul, Trench, Trubner & Co., Ltd., 1932) I, 527-573. Peter Coffey, *op. cit.,* pp. 364 ff.

[41] J. C. La Drière, Shipley's *Dictionary,* art. "Classification," p. 104.

CHAPTER II

"If Poetry Were Always Verse . . ."

In the review of Housman's lecture which Eliot wrote for *The Criterion* he stated that no critical assertion can be made without depending "upon some definition of Poetry; explicit or implicit." He prefers to keep his definition implicit because "you cannot compel anyone else to accept" it.[1] But since he admits that some definition of poetry underlies every critical statement, it should be possible with an adequate method to make such an implicit definition explicit. When forced to express what he considered was the commonly accepted explanation of the nature of "all poetry," Eliot, dissociating his statement from his own person, generalized as follows: "Everything written in verse which a sufficient number of the best minds have considered to be poetry."[2] An analysis of this reveals two pertinent conclusions: first, that this text gives no *differentia* since *poetry* is defined by the same term; and secondly, that poetry must be in verse. A passage in the "Preface" to the *Anabasis* of St.-J. Perse, a capital text in modern criticism, because in it Eliot has labored to consider his terms as carefully as possible, contradicts the second observation. To arrive at a satisfactory explanation of Eliot's *differentia* of poetry means considering the reasons for such contradictions. Therefore, beginning with the enquiry about the necessity of verse for poetry, the purpose of this study is to present Eliot's criticism as a commentary upon the following words:

> It would be convenient if poetry were always verse—
> either accented, alliterative, or quantitative; but that is
> not true. Poetry may occur, within a definite limit on one
> side, at any point along a line of which the formal
> limits are "verse" and "prose." Without offering any
> generalized theory about "poetry," "verse" and "prose,"

[1] *The Criterion*, XIII (1933-34), 153.
[2] *Use of Poetry*, p. 139.

I may suggest that a writer, by using . . . certain exclusively poetic methods, is sometimes able to write poetry in what is called prose. Another writer can, by reversing the process, write great prose in verse. There are two very simple but insuperable difficulties in any definition of "prose" and "poetry." One is that we have three terms where we need four: we have "verse" and "poetry" on the one side, and only "prose" on the other. The other difficulty follows from the first: that the words imply a valuation in one context which they do not in another. "Poetry" introduces a distinction between good verse and bad verse; but we have no one word to separate bad prose from good prose. As a matter of fact, much bad prose is poetic prose; but only a very small part of bad verse is bad because it is prosaic.[3]

This text is important because it contains most of the crucial terms to be discussed and the necessary suggestions for a methodical approach to the problem of isolating the *differentia* which Eliot attributes either explicitly or implicitly to poetry. The first sentence is simply an out-and-out contradiction of the notion that "all poetry is written in verse." In the next sentence Eliot furnishes us with the limits within which this study is confined. If poetry occurs along a line of which the formal limits are verse and prose, then the basic problem of this study is to determine Eliot's concept of the nature of this line and to show how verse and prose are related to poetry. In the explanation that follows within this passage, Eliot recognizes an awkwardness and ambiguity in the terms which he employs. Formal discourse of whatever kind, he implies, comprises a union of sound structure and meaning structure. If "certain poetic methods" are used in the meaning structure, poetry may result though the sound structure be prose. On the other hand, if the sound structure be verse but prose methods are used in the meaning structure, prose will result. There is no attempt to describe here what he means by poetic methods. Ambiguity ensues for the following reason: there is no exclusive descriptive term for the sound structure of prose. Though verse is the usual term which describes the sound structure of poetry,

---

[3] St.-J. Perse, *Anabase*, Preface to Eng. tr. by T. S. Eliot (N. Y.: Brentano's Inc., 1945), pp. [63-64]. Originally published in 1930.

the word *prose* must cover both classifications, that of sound structure and that of meaning, in the second type of discourse. Furthermore, when prose and poetry are used as evaluatory terms, poetry becomes synonymous with good verse and so the word *verse* assumes a structure of meaning. There is no such evaluatory connotation in the word *prose* applicable to the other general type of discourse. But when the derived adjectives, *poetic* and *prosaic,* are employed, *poetic* has in Eliot's use a pejorative connotation when applied to prose which is not so apparent when *prosaic* is applied to verse. Prose as a discourse is corrupted by assimilating poetic qualities; whereas verse may be judged bad, not because it is lacking in poetic qualities, but because it is deficient in prosaic virtues. As Eliot uses the word *verse* in speaking of these evaluatory connotations as well as in describing the limits of the line upon which poetry occurs, there is nothing to indicate whether he means by *verse* a structure of sound or a generic form of discourse apart from poetry and prose. Moreover, the evident alliance of poetry and prose demands an investigation of their relationship. To decide, therefore, what Eliot's concept of poetry is, the main steps of this present study must be to determine the following: first, what Eliot means by *verse;* secondly, what relationships exist between *verse* and *prose* and *poetry.* When these have been determined, it may be advisable to add a further examination of a problem they involve, viz.: the relation of *verse* to meaning.

I

The nature, the criteria for differentiation among various kinds, and the function of *verse* as Eliot conceives it, will be the problems of this chapter. Verse is the most convenient general term to designate the more or less regular patterning of rhythmic sounds in a language. As this pattern approaches regularity, an artificiality becomes more and more apparent; but this artificiality does not vitiate the integrity of the speech so fashioned in verse since in some cases this withdrawal from natural speech rhythms may be highly desirable. When Eliot says that it "would be convenient if poetry were always verse," he is confining the word *verse* in this context to structure of sound. Does he mean that verse is synonymous with meter?[4] In a very early essay are several pertinent remarks which elucidate Eliot's position quite clearly. That he does not consider verse as strict metrical pattern may be gathered from the following explanation:

> Any line can be divided into feet and accents. The simpler metres are a repetition of one combination, perhaps a long and a short, or a short and a long syllable, five times repeated. There is, however, no reason why, within the single line, there should be any repetition; why there should not be lines (as there are) divisible only into feet of different types.[5]

The complexity of centroidal patterns which is produced by the avoidance of repetition of one dominant foot not only prevents monotony but makes such verse "interesting." In practice, verse of this kind may be achieved "either by taking a very simple form, like the iambic pentameter, and constantly withdrawing from it, or taking no form at all, and constantly approximating to a very simple one. It is this contrast between fixity and flux . . . which is the very life of verse."[6]

---

[4] The term *verse* is commonly used as synonymous with *meter;* so, according to Sir Philip Hartog (*On the Relation of Poetry to Verse,* English Association Pamphlet, No. 64, London: Clarendon Press, 1926, p. 3) it is "language with a certain system of regular recurrences of sound-emphasis in it, which, for brevity, we may call 'beats,' corresponding to the beats of the conductor of a musical orchestra. The general name for such a system of beats is rhythm or metre; and the word metre is often used as a synonym of verse." In the following discussion, however, we shall find it necessary to observe a distinction not only between prose structure and verse, but between non-metrical and metrical verse. (Cf. Shipley, *Dictionary,* art. "Prosody," pp. 455-60.)

[5] "Reflections on *Vers Libre,*" *The New Statesman,* IX (Mar. 3, 1917), 518.

[6] *Ibid.,* p. 518. In the above quotation Eliot has used the word *form* to denote merely the sound structure. He employs the word in two ways; usually the context clearly denotes which meaning is intended if the reader has descriptive terms of his own into which to translate it. At times, it may mean some part of the form, in which event it may refer to structure of meaning solely: "From the point of view of literature, the drama is only one among several poetic forms." *Sac. Wood,* p. 61. Again it may signify

Here again, as in his alleged reason for avoiding a definition, is an assertion of the principle of variation between the permanent and the transitory, this time applied to sound structure and described as the "contrast between fixity and flux." In Eliot's own phrase, this is the "ghost behind the arras" of all his critical distinctions. There must be fixity of a kind, but art is achieved by the ordered withdrawal from this fixity. One must remember that Eliot formulated this principle of verse structure at the height of the controversy over "free verse."[7] Because the *vers librists* sought to do away with the fixity altogether, Eliot condemned their theory. "There is no escape from meter; there is only mastery." Consequently, *vers libre,* a battle-cry for freedom, does not exist for Eliot, largely because "there is no freedom in art . . . ; the so-called *vers libre* which is good is anything but 'free.' "[9] Verse to him, though not necessarily requiring the regularity associated with meter, cannot free itself from meter entirely.[10] Though meter represents fixity, there are two reasons that determine the use of it or the deviation from it: the first, is the language itself. Because of this Eliot holds that "some forms are more appropriate to some languages than to others."[11] And the second is a "matter

---

all form—the total complex of structural elements which make *the* form in a work, as in the following: "To create a form is not merely to invent a shape, a rhyme or rhythm. It is also the realization of the whole appropriate content of this rhyme or rhythm." *Ibid,* p. 63.

[7] For an appraisal of Eliot's contribution to this movement, see Glenn Hughes, *Imagism and the Imagists* (Stanford, Cal.: Stanford University Press, 1931), pp. 70-82.

[8] *The New Statesman.* IX (Mar. 3, 1917), p. 519.

[9] *Ibid.,* 518. Cf. *Ezra Pound* (1928), p. viii: "My own verse is, so far as I can judge, nearer to the original meaning of *vers libre* than is any of the other types: at least, the form in which I began to write in 1908 or 1909, was directly drawn from the study of Laforgue together with the later Elizabethan drama; and I do not know anyone who started from exactly that point."

[10] Cf. what Eliot has to say of meter in *Mus. of Poetry,* p. 10: "This is not to say that I consider the analytical study of metric, of the abstract forms which sound so extraordinarily different when handled by different poets, to be an utter waste of time."

[11] *Mus. of Poetry,* p. 25.

of the historical situation: at some moments a more violent change may be necessary than at others."[12]

As Eliot conceives it, therefore, *verse* is certainly not synonymous with meter. Though the suggestion of an established meter restrains the verse from slipping into indeterminateness, rigid conformity to an "abstract" pattern is not necessary. There are two directions then in which verse may oscillate. One is toward elaboration. "At some periods, the task is to explore the musical possibilities of an established convention of the relation of the idiom of verse to that of speech." The later Shakespeare and Milton exemplify this direction which verse may take. The other direction is the "task of catching up with the changes in colloquial speech."[13] If we are seeking for ghosts behind arrases, this last phrase, *colloquial speech,* is a good one to have picked. For further elucidation of Eliot's theory of verse makes it imperative to investigate the relation of *colloquial speech* to verse, if we are to understand that theory adequately.

II

One of Eliot's reasons for adhering to meter or withdrawing from it is the structure of the language itself. Certainly, he has no quarrel with English as a language.[14] But to call its principle of verse structure "a contrast between fixity and flux" is dubious descriptive terminology. Therefore, it becomes necessary to see if Eliot describes any norm of the language which will act as a stabilizing factor if verse has a necessary relation to poetry.

There can hardly be any doubt that Eliot's theory of verse in

---

[12] "In Memoriam," *Essays, Ancient and Modern* (N. Y.: Harcourt, Brace & Co., 1936), p. 176. Cf. *Mus. of Poetry,* p. 25: "At one stage the stanza is a right and natural formalization of speech into pattern. But the stanza—and the more elaborate it is, the more rules to be observed in its proper execution, the more surely this happens—tends to become fixed to the idiom of the moment of its perfection."

[13] *Mus. of Poetry,* p. 23.

[14] See "Commentary," *The Monthly Criterion,* VI (1927), 291: "Young people . . . come to understand how much the work of logicians has done to make of English a language in which it is possible to think clearly and exactly on any subject. The *Principia Mathematica* are perhaps a greater contribution to our language than they are to mathematics."

its inception, at least, is closely linked with the theories of Ezra Pound.[15] It was during the *Egoist* days that Pound published a review of Arnold Dolmetsch's *The Interpretation of the Music of the Seventeenth and Eighteenth Centuries* in which he pointed out that "poetry withers and 'dries out' when it leaves music, or at least an imagined music, too far behind it." But what was interesting Pound in this book was not music but the interpretation of the rhythms which some of the early musical theorists expounded. With a relish Pound quotes from Mace's *Musick's Monument* (1613) : ". . . you must Know, That, although in our First Undertakings, we ought to *strive,* for the most Exact Habit of *Time-Keeping* that possibly we can attain unto . . . yet, when we come to be *Masters* . . . we Then *take Liberty* . . . to *Break Time;* sometimes Faster, and sometimes Slower, as we perceive the *Nature of the Thing* Requires, which often adds, much *Grace,* and *Luster,* to the Performance." Tiring of *vers libre* ("Vers libre has become a pest. . . . It is too late to prevent [it]. It is here. There is too much of it."),[16] Pound drew from this and like quotations that the poet in his verse must employ a similar freedom in "Breaking Time." This principle he described as the "music" of poetry.[17]

---

[15] The influence of Pound upon Eliot is nowhere better exemplified than here. The extent of this influence the younger man specified in 1938 in *Purpose* (April-June, 1938), 92: "My indebtedness to Pound is of two kinds: first, in my literary criticism . . . ; and second, in his criticism of my poetry in our talks. . . . This indebtedness extends from 1915 to 1922. . . ." Cf. also the remark in *The Criterion,* XVI (1936-37), 668: "The only poet and critic who survived Imagism to develop in a larger way was Mr. Pound, who, as literary critic alone has been probably the greatest literary influence of the century up to the present time. The central importance of Mr. Pound's criticism has not yet been fully recognized." Cf. "Ezra Pound," *Poetry,* LXVIII, September 1946, 326-338.

[16] Ezra Pound, "Vers Libre and Arnold Dolmetsch," *The Egoist,* IV (1917), 90-91.

[17] Pound's interest in music dates back, as Eliot pointed out in his "Introduction" to the *Selected Poems,* p. ix, to Pound's "more antiquarian studies" where he learned "the importance of verse as song." Some of the results of these studies Pound incorporated in *The Spirit of Romance* (N. Y.: E. P. Dutton & Co., 1910) where he observed (p. 24) that "true poetry is in much closer relation to the best of music, of painting and of sculpture, than to any part of literature which is not true poetry."

In his 1917 study of Pound's verse and in subsequent discussions Eliot adopted this term. Eliot, however, was not content to repeat what Pound had written but adapted it to suit his own purposes. Thus in 1930 during a broadcast on seventeenth century poetry he pointed out that there are two kinds of music in verse. The first "that of the lyrics of Shakespeare or Campion, which *demand* the kindred music of the lute or other instrument. . . ." The second is "Donne's kind of musical verse: the verse which suggests music, but which, so to speak, contains in itself all its possible music; for if set to music, the play of ideas could not be followed. His poems are poems to be read aloud, not sung."[18] Several such remarks are scattered throughout subsequent essays, such as that in *The Use of Poetry* in which Eliot holds that "no prosodic system ever invented can teach anyone to write good English verse"; that what mattered was "the musical phrase";[19] but it is not until 1942 that there can be found a fuller explanation of the reason why Eliot adopted the term *music of poetry* to describe sound structure. From this explanation one can also see his ideas concerning the relation of the English language to verse. In English poetry, he holds, there

> is a kind of amalgam of systems of diverse sources . . .
> an amalgam like the amalgam of races, and indeed partly
> due to racial origins. The rhythms of Anglo-Saxon,
> Celtic, Norman, French, of Middle English and Scots,
> have all made their mark upon English poetry, together
> with the rhythms of Latin, and, at various periods, of
> French, Italian, and Spanish. . . .[20]

While the influence of another contemporary literature in a foreign tongue may also determine variations within the English prosodic system from time to time, the crux of the whole matter is

---

[18] "Thinking in Verse," *The Listener*, III (Mar. 1930), 442.

[19] *Use of Poetry*, p. 31. Cf. p. 57, his definition of the word *musical* in this same group of lectures: ". . . the finding of the words and the order of words expressive of the underlying mood which belongs to invention."

[20] *Mus. of Poetry*, p. 12.

in reality this: that in writing verse there is a law of nature which must never be violated: and that law is

> that poetry must not stray too far from the ordinary everyday language which we use and hear. Whether poetry is accentual or syllabic, rhymed or rhymeless, formal or free, it cannot afford to lose its contact with the changing language of common intercourse.[21]

Therefore, what Eliot, following Pound, calls *music,* is partly the rhythms of the poet's speech. "Poetry . . . remains . . . one person talking to another; and this is just as true if you sing it, for singing is another way of talking."[22] Not only is the poet permitted, but it is his "business to use the speech which he finds about him, and that with which he is most familiar." Not that he is limited in the theoretical Wordsworthian sense to the speech of any class.[23] The poet is not expected to "reproduce exactly the conversational idiom of himself, his family, and his particular district: but what he finds there is the material out of which he must make his poetry."[24] By emphasizing this use of colloquial speech, Eliot does not mean that the speech of his poetry and the speech of the poet as a social individual are exactly the same; but,—once more a fixity-flux contrast is established—"it has to be in such a

---

[21] *Ibid.,* p. 13.

[22] *Ibid.,* p. 16.

[23] Cf. *Use of Poetry,* p. 72: ". . . it is not the business of the poet to talk like *any* class of society, but like himself—rather better, we hope, than any actual class; though when any class of society happens to have the best word, phrase or expletive for anything, then the poet is entitled to it."

[24] *Mus. of Poetry,* p. 16. Cf. *The Criterion,* XIV (1934-35), 611: "It is not a matter of indifference that poetry written by an Irishman, a Welshman, a Scot, an American or a Jew should be indistinguishable from that written by an Englishman: it is undesirable. . . . It is not a petty question of employing one's native Doric, which is merely a nuisance, except for an occasional word or phrase which may enrich the English language; it is not a question of being sentimental about the old homestead and the landscapes of childhood. What is essentially Scottish about Dunbar is not his vocabulary; and what is essentially American about Walt Whitman is not his admiration for New York or for the vast size of his country. What is essential is impossible fully to define, but it is most effectually expressed through rhythm."

relation to the speech of his time that the listener or reader can say 'that is how I should talk if I could talk poetry.' "[25]

It is only when we understand Eliot's insistence upon the necessity for incorporating the rhythms of contemporary speech into verse and the necessary modifications which this brings about in the sound structure that we can appreciate his casual remark in the essay on *Anabase*: "As a matter of fact much bad prose is poetic prose; but only a very small part of bad verse is bad because it is prosaic," and realize that in this context he is referring to structure of sound as it is determined by the colloquial and the general grammatical development of sentence structure. This clarifies some of his contexts in which the idea of the *prosaic* is used, such as the following: "Certain qualities are to be expected of any type of good verse at any time; we may say the qualities which good verse shares with good prose."[26]

One reason why most of the productions of the eighteenth century "after Pope, Swift, Prior, and Gay," are bad, is that the writers did not work on the principle of fitness but continued to use sound structures which were not appropriate for what they wished to say. They did not inform verse with prose virtues. Not adapting their sound structures to their new meaning structures, they continued to use sound structures which were popular but ill-fitted to the new meanings.

How important this quality of perfect pliability of sound structure is to Eliot may be judged from his statement that Goldsmith's and Johnson's verse is "poetry partly because it has the virtues of

---

[25] *Mus. of Poetry*, p. 16.

[26] "Johnson's 'London' and 'Vanity,'" *English Critical Essays of the Twentieth Century*, ed. P. M. Jones (London: Oxford University Press, 1933), pp. 303-304. As Eliot says, the word *prose* is ambiguous, and his use of it demands interpretation according to the context. His most customary use of it is as an evaluatory term applied to sound structure as that is determined by the general contour of the sentence structure. *Good prose* for Eliot usually means well-constructed sentences. And he holds that the sentences of poetry should be just as "well-written" as those of any other type of discourse. Throughout the essay on Johnson this seems to be his meaning. Cf. his judgment on Dryden, p. 306 and the following on Johnson: "And the verse of Johnson has the good qualities of his own best prose, and of the best prose of his time." P. 309.

good prose."[27] Approximation to prose cadences, rather than the
repetition of the same metrical unit, makes the verse flexible and
malleable. Since prose and verse have common problems of expression, "a poet can learn essential knowledge from the study of the
best prose"; so that "prose which has *nothing* in common with
verse is dead; verse which has nothing in common with prose is
probably artificial, false, diffuse, and syntactically weak."[28]

Because of the nature of the English language, the diversity of
linguistic elements which contribute to its richness, Eliot recognized the insufficiency of traditional prosodic systems to account
for the variety and charm of the rhythms of English poetry. To
describe the complexity of the sound structures which he perceived
in his medium and also to legitimize the variations which he
wished to introduce into his own work, he, following the lead of
Ezra Pound, attempted to link them with music. However, seeing
that this liaison was not completely satisfactory, he modified the
conception of *music* to include the rhythms of colloquial speech.
This then is the norm for verse rhythms. As a norm for poetry
it is too nebulous and too suggestive of prose rhythms to supply
a characterizing note for poetry unless some sharp distinctions
can be made in the differentiation of the various kinds of verse;
and it is to this problem that we shall next turn.

III

"It may appear strange," Eliot wrote in 1942, "that when I
profess to be talking about the 'music' of poetry, I put such
emphasis upon conversation. But I would remind you, first, that
the music of poetry is not something which exists apart from the
meaning."[29] What matters is the unity of the whole work. Ezra
Pound had expanded his ideas on form in an article in the *Egoist*
and part of this Eliot quoted in his early study of Pound:

> Any work of art is a compound of freedom and order.
> It is perfectly obvious that art hangs between chaos

---

[27] *Ibid.,* p. 304.
[28] *John Dryden, the Poet, the Dramatist, the Critic* (N. Y.: Terence &
Elsa Holliday, 1932), p. 44.
[29] *Mus. of Poetry,* p. 13.

> on one side and mechanics on the other. . . . A pedantic
> insistence on detail tends to drive out "major form." A
> firm hold on major form makes for freedom of detail.
> . . . Art is a departure from fixed positions; felicitous
> departure from a norm.[30]

"Major form" is Pound's term for total structure. If one of the
details of a work is too mechanical in its adjustment to the others,
Pound avers, the perfect harmony of the whole structure is
destroyed. Pound's "adaptability of metre to mood" Eliot extolled
and called it his *music*.[31]

The controversy over free verse, as Eliot was later to write, was
important for just this reason: it represented a "revolt against
dead form."[32] The exponents of free verse insisted that the unity
of the individual work was of greater moment than conformity
to a typical unity of prosodic pattern. The principle which determines the structure of sound, therefore, is fitness. "Without this
fitness, which is contingent upon period as well as individual
genius, the rest is at best virtuosity. . . ."[33] Nice discrimination in
perceiving this adjustment of sound and meaning is not always
forthcoming from the average reader. "People," Eliot wrote in
1928,

> may think they like the form because they like the con-
> tent, or think they like the content because they like the
> form. In the perfect poet they fit and are the same thing;
> and in another sense they *always* are the same thing. So
> it is always true to say that form and content are the
> same thing, and always true to say that they are different
> things.[34]

But the serious artist is always conscious of his efforts toward
perfect integration. "I am accustomed to the search for form: but

---

[30] "Arnold Dolmetsch," *The Egoist,* IV (1917), 104-105.

[31] *Ezra Pound* (1917), p. 7.

[32] In a short retrospective comment in *The Criterion,* XVI (1936-37),
668, Eliot emphasized the importance of the Imagist movement and enumer-
ated the major influences which contributed to making that sporadic effort
significant.

[33] *Mus. of Poetry,* p. 25. Cf. Dryden's "Preface to Sylvae," *Essays,* ed.
W. P. Ker (Oxford: Clarendon Press, 1926), I, p. 255.

[34] *Ezra Pound* (1928), p. x.

Kipling never seems to be searching for form, but only for a
particular form for each poem."[35] Searching for form is a seeking
for structural elements which, when combined, will unite to make
a unique work. Thus there must always be a constant interaction
between the structure of sound and the structure of meaning. One
influences the other and the perfection of the work is achieved
only if there is perfect conformity of all elements.[36] Eliot summed
up his thoughts on this matter excellently in *The Music of Poetry*
when he wrote:

> As for "free verse," I expressed my view twenty-five
> years ago by saying that no verse is free for the man
> who wants to do a good job. Only a bad poet could wel-
> come free verse as a liberation from form. It was a re-
> volt against dead form, and a preparation for new form
> or for the renewal of the old: it was an insistence upon
> the inner unity which is typical.[37]

The beauty of a work for Eliot must depend upon this "inner
unity." Perhaps one reason why he has emphasized this union so
much is that for him " 'verbal beauty' is probably never, in literature, a beauty of *pure* sound; I doubt whether there is a beauty
of pure sound."[38] This was written in 1921. Much later, he explained that within its own language it is doubtful that any word
"is more or less beautiful than another" from the standpoint of
sound alone. Therefore, for Eliot, the "music" of a word (and
therefore its beauty) is not an absolute quality within the sound
itself but arises at an intersection between two relations: one, with
the "words immediately preceding and following it, and indefinitely
to the rest of its context"; and the second from "its immediate

---

[35] *A Choice of Kipling's Verse* (N. Y.: Charles Scribner's Sons, 1942),
p. 16. See also *Mus. of Poetry*, p. 28.

[36] As an instance of this Eliot cites the fact that using a quantitative
measure, as some of Pound's poems do, "lays so heavy a burden upon
every word in a line" that haphazard composition, such as leaving blanks
for adjectives, as Shelley sometimes did, or making adjectives so general
that they are "practically blanks," is virtually prohibited. *Ezra Pound*
(1917), p. 12.

[37] *Mus. of Poetry*, p. 26.

[38] "Prose and Verse," *The Chapbook*, No. 22 (1921), 7.

meaning in that context to its greater or less wealth of association."[39] For Eliot then, the " 'musical poem' . . . has a musical
pattern of sound and a musical pattern of the secondary meanings
of the words which compose it . . . and these two patterns are indissoluble and one." For this reason he considers that "the sound
of a poem is as much an abstraction from the poem as is the
sense."[40]

Since the sound structure is so integral a part of the total structure of a poem, it is just as important as the meanings to Eliot.[41]
Consequently, in the genesis of a work it may appear first, a fact
which Eliot has noted several times throughout his later writings.
In *The Music of Poetry* he declared that

> a poem, or a passage of a poem, may tend to realize itself
> first as a particular rhythm before it reaches expression
> in words, and that this rhythm may bring to birth the
> idea and the image; and I do not believe that this is an
> experience peculiar to myself.[42]

How important verse rhythm is to Eliot is summed up when he
described it as "the real pattern in the carpet, the scheme of organization of thought, feeling, and vocabulary, the way in which

---

[39] *Mus. of Poetry,* pp. 18-19.

[40] *Ibid.,* p. 19. Eliot's use of the term *music* as a descriptive one is not
confined, as it generally is in poetic theory, to the sound alone or to the
rhythm alone or to a combination of these. His use of it includes meaning
and, therefore, music is equivalent to the unity of the work; the poem is
more or less beautiful according to the greater or less degree of unity which
is apparent in it.

[41] Cf. Hopkins' definition of poetry and his stress on the structural importance of sound: "Poetry is speech framed for contemplation of the mind
by the way of hearing or speech framed to be heard for its own sake and
interest even over and above its interest of meaning." This definition appeared in *The Criterion,* XV (1935-36), 11, when some early poems and
extracts were published from the *Notebooks and Papers.*

[42] *Mus. of Poetry,* p. 28. A similar description is given in *A Choice of
Kipling's Verse, op. cit.,* p. 18. For another description of the way poetry
may be written, see *Use of Poetry,* pp. 144-145. Cf. also what Hopkins says
about "The Wreck of the *Deutschland," Letters,* II, ed. C. C. Abbott
(London: Oxford University Press, 1935), p. 14.

everything comes together."[43] But the rhythm of good verse is not
only colloquial; it is personally colloquial. "Rhythm," Eliot continued in this note on Marianne Moore, ". . . is a highly personal
matter; it is not a verse-form. It is very uncommon. . . . That
quality is something which no system of scansion can define."[44]

For Eliot the great exemplar of this personal rhythm is, of
course, Donne. His insertion of a "conversational tone in his
poetry, which is a matter of choice and arrangement of words . . .
makes one feel that Donne is himself speaking to you personally
and familiarly, although speaking great poetry."[45] That is what
constitutes Dryden's greatness as a poet: it was impossible for
him to "write an artificial style. . . . What Dryden did in fact was
to reform the language, and devise a natural, conversational style
of speech in verse in place of an artificial and decadent one."[46]

Verse has its foundation in the colloquial speech of the poet.
The rhythm of the speech to which he is accustomed is the basis
for the sound structure which he must use if he is to produce even
satisfactory poetry. But to differentiate his poetry from that of
others, to make significant work, the poet must introduce a rhythm

---

[43] *The Dial,* LXXV (1923), 595.

[44] For other texts which emphasize this element of personal rhythm, see
Sel. Essays, p. 192 and p. 199; and "Commentary," *The Criterion,* III
(1924-25), 343.

[45] "Rhyme and Reason," *The Listener,* III, 503. See also *John Dryden*
(1932), p. 12; *A Garland for John Donne,* ed. Theodore Spencer (Cambridge: Harvard University Press, 1931), p. 14, p. 16, and p. 17; "John
Donne," *The Nation & The Athenaeum* (June 9, 1923), 332.

[46] *John Dryden* (1932), p. 10. Donne and Dryden, though not the only
ones of whom Eliot has spoken as possessing this intimate verse rhythm,
are the two he thinks who accomplished the revolutions and reforms of language when they were needed. See *ibid.,* "The Poet," *passim; Sel. Essays,*
p. 459; "Introduction" to *The Collected Poems of Harold Monro,* ed. Alida
Monro (London: Cobden-Sanderson, 1933), p. xvi; and "Preface" to
Selected Poems by Marianne Moore, ed. T. S. Eliot (London: Faber &
Faber, 1935), p. 7. That this intimacy of rhythm is not confined to verse
goes without saying. Contrasting Henry James with Milton, Eliot noted
that "the sound, of course, is never irrelevant, and the style of James certainly depends for its effect a good deal on the sound of a voice, James'
own, painfully explaining. . . ." "Note on the verse of John Milton," *Essays
and Studies of the English Association* (London: Clarendon Press, 1936),
XXI, p. 36.

which is exclusively indicative of him. This quality makes his work outstanding; it differentiates it from other verse of the same kind and gives it rarity and distinction.[47] "What is poetic about poetry is just the invention or discovery or elaboration of a new idiom in verse," Eliot stated in his broadcast on "John Dryden."[48] Idiom, of course, belongs to meanings; but it is idiom which determines the individual rhythm and thus influences the personal music of verse. What every poet should constantly strive to achieve is the introduction of this personal rhythm into his work. It is for this that he must experiment. This is one of the primary reasons why he must know what other poets have done. Otherwise, he will merely parody or repeat them.[49]

To achieve this personal rhythm, there is a natural gift that Eliot mentions as necessary for the poet to possess if he is to be "sensitive to" the "musical qualities of verse." This gift, the "auditory imagination," he defines as

> the feeling for syllable and rhythm, penetrating far below the conscious levels of thought and feeling, invigorating every word; sinking to the most primitive and for-

---

[47] Delmore Schwartz, one of Eliot's most enthusiastic and penetrating interpreters (See "T. S. Eliot as the International Hero," *Partisan Review,* XII, Spring, 1945, 199-206) remarked in his review of *Four Quartets* (*The Nation,* CLVII, July 24, 1943, 102) upon the way Eliot's theory in this matter has been conscientiously carried over into his practice. For unenthusiastic interpretation of Eliot's rhythms, see Y. Winters, *Primitivism and Decadence* (Norfolk, Conn.: New Directions, 1939), *passim* and A. Guérard, *Robert Bridges* (Cambridge: Harvard University Press, 1942).

[48] *The Listener,* III (Apr. 16, 1930), 689.

[49] Cf. the essay on *Ezra Pound* (1928), p. xxi: "I remember that Pound once induced me to destroy what I thought an excellent set of couplets; for, said he, 'Pope has done this so well that you cannot do it better; and if you mean this as a burlesque, you had better suppress it, for you cannot parody Pope unless you can write better verse than Pope—and you can't!'" "For a poet to do what has been done already," Eliot wrote in 1918, is as wasteful "as for a biologist to rediscover Mendel's discoveries" ("Contemporanea," *The Egoist,* V, 1918, 84). Failure to know or realize what has been achieved may result in useless repetition; and Eliot wrote much later that "no first-rate poet would attempt to do again, what has already been done as well as it can be done in his language." *What Is a Classic?* (London: Faber & Faber, 1944), p. 24.

> gotten, returning to the origin and bringing something
> back, seeking the beginning and the end. It works through
> meanings, certainly, or not without meanings in the ordi-
> nary sense, and fuses the old and obliterated and the trite,
> the current, and the new and surprising, the most
> ancient and the most civilized mentality.[50]

Not only then must the poet possess wide intellectual knowledge of his art, but he must also possess a kind of affective knowledge (since the auditory imagination is described as "the feeling
for syllable and rhythm") which mingles with his cognitions to
effect the work he is making. The fusion of these two knowledges
is the means whereby the poet may produce that personal rhythm
which will set his verse apart from the verse of all other writers.
Its function is to cement all the formal elements in the poem. Not
only must the rhythm unite with vocabulary and thought; it must
also combine with affectivity. It is this combination, in Eliot's
opinion, which makes the music of Pound so notable: Pound's
verse is always definite and concrete, because he has always a
definite emotion behind it.[51] Structure of sound is musical when
it is united with structure of meaning but meaning to be poetically
effective must be not only cognitive but also affective. Eliot also
speaks of this blending of structural elements in the essay on the
metaphysical poets where affectivity is again closely linked with
cognitive meaning and sound. The sentence structure of Donne
and of the other poets of the metaphysical school, though far from
simple, is nevertheless faithful "to thought and feeling. . . . And as
this fidelity induces variety of thought and feeling, so it induces
variety of music."[52]
From these statements it would seem that what makes the "tones"
particular or the "rhythms" personal or the "music" varied, is
just this coalescing of rhythm with affectivity. Since this rhythm
is personal and engendered by the auditory imagination of the

---

[50] *Use of Poetry,* pp. 118-119. Cf. de Gourmont, *Le Problème,* pp. 41-42
for a somewhat similar description of the function of rhythm. T. E. Hulme
(*Speculations,* ed. Herbert Read, London: Kegan Paul, Trench, Trubner
& Co., 1924, pp. 155-157) also has some interesting observations on rhythm.
[51] *Ezra Pound* (1917), p. 13.
[52] *Sel. Essays,* p. 285. See also *ibid.,* p. 119.

poet, when this personal rhythm appears in verse, it is an important part of what is expressed in the total structure. With an understanding of the importance which Eliot attributes to the affective meaning which the rhythm conveys, it is not surprising to read in the essay on Dante "that genuine poetry can communicate before it is understood."[53] If the words are not understood, then the poetry cannot convey specific intellectual cognitions. If communication takes place by means of the sound and rhythm, whatever is communicated must be either an indefinite cognitive or an affective meaning. To the latter Eliot assented when he noted: "I have found with Dante and with several other poets in languages in which I was unskilled, that about such impressions there was nothing fanciful . . . the impression was new, and of, I believe the objective 'poetic emotion.' "[54]

In summary, then, Eliot conceives *verse* to be a patterning of sound upon the colloquial speech of the poet. Verse is differentiated by the appearance of a personal rhythm which individualizes that poet's work. This individuality is achieved largely through a sensibility which responds to affective stimuli. It is possible that verse so conceived may have some necessary relation to poetry, such as the relation of one affective stimulus to a complex of affective and cognitional stimuli. The rhythm acts as a cohesive force in organizing the other stimuli into a unified musical structure. It is possible that verse may be the medium for communicating an affective meaning. To see whether in fact Eliot thinks there is such necessary relation between verse and poetry the next chapter will examine the sound structure of prose and poetry to determine whether the *differentia* of poetry for Eliot lies in sound structure.

---

[53] *Sel. Essays,* p. 238.
[54] *Ibid.,* p. 238. Cf. also p. 118; and *Use of Poetry,* p. 62.

CHAPTER III

Insuperable Difficulties

1. Structure of Sound in Prose and Poetry

Though *verse* apparently bears a relation to poetry for Eliot, particularly as an affective stimulus, still he has specified that "it is not true" that poetry is always in verse. Furthermore, since he has written that poetry may "occur within a definite limit on one side at any point along a line of which the formal limits are 'verse' and 'prose,' " it becomes necessary before any conclusion can be drawn about placing the *differentia* in the sound structure to see what relation is to be found between *verse* and *poetry* and *prose*. Eliot's declaration in the "Preface" to *Anabasis* that poetry need not necessarily be constructed in verse is contradicted by what he said in 1917:

> There are doubtless many empirical generalisations which one may draw from a study of existing poetry and prose, but after much reflection I conclude that the only absolute distinction to be drawn is that poetry is written in verse, and prose is written in prose; or, in other words, that there is prose rhythm and verse rhythm. And any essential difference is still to seek.[1]

Eliot's concept of verse is so flexible that it would permit much margin for freedom of structure. But the positiveness of his assertion in the above quotation makes it necessary to seek some resolution for the problem presented. This contradiction might be extenuated on the ground that these quotations are in two different contexts and, since so much of Eliot's work is published in an ephemeral form and since he does not look upon himself as a professional critic but only as a poet writing about poetry,[2] too

---

[1] "The Borderline of Prose," *The New Statesman*, IX (May 19, 1917), 158.

[2] See *supra*, p. 5, note 19.

exact a consistency should not be demanded of him. But care-
lessness cannot be postulated of either of the sources from which
these texts are taken.[3] And secondly, whether he looks upon himself as a professional critic or not, Eliot's position has been so
prominent that his work cannot escape close scrutiny from students
of contemporary literature. Furthermore, he has laid so much
importance upon sound structure in his work that such a deviation
would seem to be a capital point to treat in attempting to isolate
his *differentia* of poetry. Therefore, if in one text it is located in
the sound structure and if in another text it is removed from this
position, such ambiguity demands investigation. If this property
cannot be isolated on the level of sound structure by a resolution
of the contradictions inherent in these statements, the search for
a *differentia* must be carried further.

As mediums of discourse, Eliot asserts that verse and prose are
equally important; both may require equal care in composition.
Likewise, "any enjoyment that can be communicated by verse may
be communicated by prose, with the exception of the pleasure of
metrical form." And even this last is offset by the "movement of
the finest prose, which is peculiar to prose and cannot be com-
pensated by verse."[4]

But in seeking to differentiate prose and poetry, twice Eliot has
noted that literary theory needs a "fourth term." Of the "two very

---

[3] The "Preface" to the *Anabasis* was obviously written with the care and
consideration Eliot would give to a work that he had taken the trouble to
translate; and "The Borderline of Prose" was one of the first articles on
literary criticism that he published. It was a refutation of some of the dog-
matic assertions of the Imagists and must have been formulated after delib-
erate reflection.

[4] *The Chapbook,* No. 22 (1921), 4. The difficulty of seeking the *differentia*
of poetry exclusively in the final cause or on the basis of the pleasure to be
derived from it was clearly recognized quite early by Eliot. "It proves impossible," he wrote in this same essay, ". . . to draw any line between . . .
those works the chief aim or effect of which is aesthetic pleasure, and those
which give aesthetic pleasure in the production of some other effect." This
remark shows that Eliot recognizes that the nature of pleasure is not sufficiently differentiated to determine satisfactorily the essential nature of
poetry. Furthermore, the rhetorical treatises had provided for pleasure as one
of the three major *officia* or functions of the orator. See Cicero, *Orator,* 76-
112; St. Augustine, *Doct. Christ.* 4, 34; Quintilian, *Institutes,* III, iv. 1-2.

simple but insuperable difficulties" that he spoke of in the *Ana-basis* as present in "any definition of 'prose' and 'poetry,' " the one that is important for the present discussion is "that we have three terms where we need four; we have 'verse' and 'poetry' on the one side and only 'prose' on the other." This demand for a fourth term was not a new idea in Eliot's criticism in 1929. In "Prose and Verse," while trying to make a distinction between the prose of Gibbon and De Quincey and the poetry of Poe and Dryden, Eliot raised the same complaint: "Thus we might fairly say that we need a fourth term: we have the term 'verse' and the term 'poetry' and only the term 'prose' to express their opposites."[5] Verse is usually associated with poetry as its designation for sound structure, but the one term, *prose,* must do double duty. It must signify the sound structure in prose cadences and also the generic form of discourse. Eliot had said in the *Anabasis*: "Without offering any generalized theory about 'poetry,' 'verse,' and 'prose,' I may suggest that a writer, by using . . . certain exclusively poetic methods, is some-times able to write poetry in what is called prose. Another writer can, by reversing the process, write great prose in verse."[6] It is the traditional association of verse with poetry which Eliot would seem to wish to dissolve, thus supporting what he had said in *The Chapbook*: "I do not assume the identification of poetry with verse." To avoid ambiguity, Eliot declares that we need a fourth term to designate poetry in the sound structure of prose. With the needed term, cross references between sound and meaning struc-tures could be achieved unequivocally. Thus, a work, whether written in prose or verse, could be denominated poetry if its struc-ture of meaning had been achieved by using "certain exclusively poetic methods." On the other hand, prose would be prose (even though written in verse) if its meaning structure required that term.[7]

---

[5] *The Chapbook,* No. 22 (1921), *loc. cit.,* 4.

[6] What Eliot means by "exclusively poetic methods" is discussed in section three of this chapter.

[7] The consequences of this would be that no structure of meaning, such as the novel or essay, would be limited to one sound structure. A work, such as Mr. James Joyce's *Ulysses* then would not be condemned "on the ground that it is 'poetry' and therefore should have been written in verse," when,

In order to reconcile this theory with that expressed in 1917, that "poetry is written in verse and prose is written in prose," it must be recalled that Eliot wrote the latter as he was entering the controversy over prose-poetry. What the Imagists called the *prose-poem*, Eliot repudiated for various reasons, but chiefly because he objected to their treatment of sound structure in the works they published. He objected to Aldington's prose-poems, for instance, upon the principle that they hesitated between two media; this hesitation, he declared, is fatal to the "necessary articulation of rhythm." Prose-poems fail "because they seek to evade the technical distinctions between two forms."[8] Eliot contended that there is a "prose arbitrariness and a verse arbitrariness" which demand a compliance to the limitations of the medium chosen; any attempt to confuse these structures only results in failure of unity in the whole structure. What matters is the inevitableness of the sound structure chosen. If the lack of inevitability in the sound structure causes the reader to imagine how this work would sound in some other medium, the unity which should dominate the work is lost, and so neither good prose nor good poetry is obtained. No matter what the subjects may be, if the structures are such that "they seem to have come to their author already clothed in that

---

for Eliot, it is the "most vital development of prose that has taken place in this generation" (*The Chapbook*, 1921, p. 10). If the fourth term had been available perhaps less circumlocution would have been necessary in Eliot's description of *Nightwood* (*The Criterion*, XVI, 1936-37, 561) : "In describing *Nightwood* for the purpose of attracting readers to the English edition, I said that it would 'appeal primarily to readers of poetry.' . . . I do not want to suggest that the distinction of the book is primarily verbal, and still less that the astonishing language covers a vacuity of content. . . . And I do not mean that Miss Barnes's style is 'poetic prose.' . . . A prose that is altogether alive demands something of the reader that the ordinary novel-reader is not prepared to give. To say that *Nightwood* will appeal primarily to readers of poetry does not mean that it is not a novel, but that it is so good a novel than only sensibilities trained on poetry can wholly appreciate it." The ambiguity which results in calling persons poets who construct works of art in prose sound structure, Eliot tried to avoid by using the term *man of letters*. See "The Man of Letters and the Future of Europe," *Sewanee Review*, LIII (1945), 333; *Sel. Essays*, p. 160; and the introduction to *Bubu of Montparnasse*, tr. Laurence Vail (Paris: Crosby Continental Editions, 1932), p. x.

[8] *The New Statesman*, IX (May 19, 1917), 159.

form," then that structure is right for them. The important thing
is that the work should not suggest an alternative mode. Dante in
describing the Aristotelian soul is not "prosaic," nor is Rimbaud in his works less "poetic" for not writing in verse.[9] Eliot
does not deny that both Dante and Rimbaud wrote poetry, though
one wrote in verse and the other in prose. This statement appeared in the same essay as the declaration that "poetry is written
in verse and prose is written in prose." Therefore, what Eliot was
trying to emphasize in this context was not that verse must always
be the sound structure of poetry, but that if poetry uses verse, it
must not attempt to use the sound structure of prose also.[10] By confusing sound structures the writers of prose poetry failed to produce works in which the various elements were so intertwined
that the result possessed "inner necessity."

In terms of the concept of poetry, then, we may conclude from
these texts that the *differentia* of poetry for Eliot does not rest in
the sound structure since poetry may occur in prose or verse.

But while he has said most emphatically, "I do not assume the
identification of poetry with verse; good poetry is obviously something else besides good verse; and good verse may be very indifferent poetry,"[11] there is no denying that for him poetry has a
natural affinity for verse. If the verse form is "impeccable and
inevitable" as in some of Pope's works, he maintained in 1917, this
may make "permanent poetry of the prosaic."[12] "No one," Eliot
wrote in the "Introduction" to *Ezra Pound*, "is competent to judge

---

[9] Studying in this context Eliot's use of the adjectives *poetic* and *prosaic*,
one sees that he is using them as evaluatory not as descriptive terms. (This
is the second of the reasons which he lists in the "Preface" to the *Anabasis*
for the insuperable difficulties which hinder a precise definition of prose and
poetry.) But this evaluation is made not in terms of sound structure but in
terms of meaning structure. If one calls prose *poetic*, that does not mean
that "the prose is aspiring to verse"; neither by calling verse *prosaic* would
the verse "be [made] any less contemptible in prose." *Ibid.*, pp. 158-159.

[10] Cf. *The Chapbook*, No. 22, *loc. cit.*, 5: "A single work must have some
metrical unity. This may vary widely in practice: I see no reason why a
considerable variety of verse forms may not be employed within the limits
of a single poem; or why a prose writer should not vary his cadences almost
indefinitely."

[11] *Ibid.*, p. 3.

[12] *The New Statesman*, IX (May 19, 1917), 158.

poetry until he recognizes that poetry is nearer to 'verse' than it is to prose poetry."[13] Even in the "Preface" he intimated that though the *Anabasis* might be "called prose, its declamation, the system of stresses and pauses, which is partially exhibited by the punctuation and spacing, is that of poetry and not of prose."[14] His preference for poetry in verse may be deduced from *The Use of Poetry*, where after referring to a variety of "kinds," he concluded: "All the kinds seem to have nothing in common except the rhythm of verse instead of the rhythm of prose," and this "does not tell you much about all poetry."[15]

Even though Eliot thinks that the differentiating quality of poetry is something else besides the sound structure, the kind of poetry he prefers and the kind that he thinks of when he generalizes about "all poetry," is poetry that is written in verse. This, however, does not give us the *differentia* that will separate poetry from every other discourse. In order to seek this quality the next consideration must be what Eliot thinks is the difference between the meanings of poetry and the meanings of prose.

2. MEANINGS IN PROSE AND POETRY

In Eliot's criticism the word *form* has two uses. He employs it to signify the total structure of a work. Then again, he applies it to sound structure alone. When form functions in the latter sense, it is usually combined with another term to denote or describe another element which unites to make a discourse. At times, this term is

---

[13] *Ezra Pound* (1928), p. xix.

[14] *Anabase, op. cit.,* p. 61. Cf. (!) Hugh Gordon Porteus' remark on *The Waste Land*: "It is in verse, but that is no matter. Mr. Eliot has somewhere observed that the only important distinction between prose and verse lies in their use of different systems of punctuation." *Wyndham Lewis* (London: Desmond Harmsworth, 1932), p. 144.

[15] *Use of Poetry*, p. 155. Speaking of Byron in 1937 and admitting that "he added nothing to the language, that he discovered nothing in the sound, and developed nothing in the meaning, of individual words," Eliot seemed to be at a loss to find a reason why Byron is a poet except that he possessed "a torrential fluency of verse and a skill in varying it from time to time to avoid monotony." "Byron," *From Anne to Victoria,* ed. B. Dobrée (N. Y.: Charles Scribner's Sons, 1937), p. 605.

"content"; again it is "matter." But because this member changes
and because it has varying explanations, some of these terms must
be scrutinized to determine what else besides sound Eliot recognizes
as making the total structure of a work. Not the least startling of
these combinations is the yoking of "form" with "significance of
feeling" or simply with "feeling."[16] Effort toward technical excellence, Eliot says, helps a poet to prepare a medium "for the
moment when he really has something to say." When the medium
and the technique converge at the proper moment, something results in which medium and material . . . are indistinguishable."[17]

From these two quotations one can see that what causes difficulty ultimately for a clear discussion of form is that meaning is
not specifically mentioned. At times, it is "something to say,"
which may be roughly equated with meaning; but at others, it is
"significance of feeling,"—an affective term which involves many
problems. In discussing the structural elements of poetry in 1935
Eliot pointed to two constituents—one of which is emotion—when
he declared: ". . . a precise fitness of form and matter mean also
a balance between them: thus the form, the pattern movement,
has a solemnity of its own . . . however light and gay the human
emotion concerned."[18] Form, as Eliot used it here, was of course,
the sound structure. The other structuralizing factor mentioned
is emotion. If this had been casually introduced once, it might be
dismissed, but terms of affectivity appear at all the crucial points

---

[16] *Ezra Pound* (1928), p. xxi Cf. also the following, p. xxii: "But if we
really love poetry, then we know and must know all its degrees. The distinction between technique and feeling—a distinction necessarily arbitrary
and brutal—will not bother us: we shall be able to appreciate what is good
of its kind; we shall be able to appreciate the meeting of the peaks, the
fusion of matter and means, form and content, on any level. . . ." And p. xv:
"In *Ripostes* and *Lustra,* there are many short poems of a slighter build
than this, equally moving, but in which also the 'feeling' or 'mood' is more
interesting than the writing. (In the perfect poem, both are equally interesting, and being equally interesting are interesting as one thing and not as
two.)" See also *A Choice of Kipling's Verse,* p. 8: ". . . but neither in
feeling nor in rhythm does most of it give any hint that the author would
ever write a memorable poem."
[17] *Ezra Pound* (1928), pp. xx-xxi.
[18] *Marianne Moore* (1935), pp. 11-12.

of discussion, so that every such emphasis upon affectivity becomes of the highest significance.

However, Eliot has referred to "content" and "matter"; when we turn to the question whether there is any difference in the subject-matter of poetry from that of prose, we see that quite early Eliot asserted that distinction between poetry and prose was not a question of subject-matter. Rather it is the way "in which this subject-matter is treated."[19] This implies a distinction in the manner in which meaning functions in the two discourses. If this functional difference involves a real distinction, then a specific differentia must somehow be implied.

I

Eliot states a relation between poetry and other intellectual activities in the 1928 Preface to *The Sacred Wood*: "Poetry . . . has something to do with morals, and with religion, and even with politics perhaps, though we cannot say what."[20] But if Eliot cannot state how far other disciplines encroach upon poetry, he has made many pronouncements protesting what might be termed illegitimate uses to which the meaning of poetry has been put. As these protests state emphatically that certain values cannot be found in poetry, it is necessary to take cognizance of them before finding out positively what the poet's purpose actually is. Because Eliot has been so largely concerned with evaluating poetry in his criticism, and because this study is primarily engaged with poetry, there is little here that relates directly to the function of prose. That function is rather to be inferred from the argument of what poetry is not supposed to do.

Eliot objects to using poetry for the purpose of deriving values which should be obtained from other activities. The most generalized statement of his view appears in *The Use of Poetry*, but there are many other formulations in other essays:

> . . . nothing in this world or the next is a substitute for
> anything else; and if you find that you must do without

---

[19] *The Chapbook*, No. 22 (1921), 3.
[20] *Sac. Wood*, p. x.

something, such as religious faith or philosophic belief, then you must just do without it. I can persuade myself, I find, that some of the things that I can hope to get are better worth having than some of the things I cannot get; or I may hope to alter myself so as to want different things; but I cannot persuade myself that it is the same desires that are satisfied, or that I have in effect the same thing under a different name.[21]

This tendency toward the substitution of poetic for other values, Eliot finds first in Wordsworth. In Johnson's relatively settled society, "poetry was still poetry, and not another thing."[22] The functions of the various disciplines were clearly defined and dynamically operative within their own sphere. In the chaotic world of Wordsworth, however, the poet began "to annex new authority . . . to meddle with social affairs, and to offer a new kind of religious sentiment" which it seemed his unique privilege to expound.[23] With Shelley "we are struck from the beginning by the number of things poetry is expected to do."[24] By the time we arrive at Arnold the substitution of poetry for religion is complete. Eliot describes Arnold's accomplishing this sleight-of-hand by dismissing the intellectual element in religion and by demanding that literary art inculcate morality. "It is only a short step, if any

---

[21] *Use of Poetry,* pp. 113-114. The reason for this "substitution" Eliot attributes to general intellectual confusion and the disintegration of culture. In *The Criterion,* II (1923-24), 373, he made the following comment: "Of all these tendencies toward obliteration of distinctions, the most dangerous is the tendency to confuse literature with religion—a tendency which can only have the effect of degrading literature and annihilating religion. This particular heresy has lately been dealt with very ably by M. Jacques Rivière in an article in *La Nouvelle Revue Française* on 'The Crisis of the Concept of Literature.' " For other statements on this "substitution," see *Sel. Essays,* p. 44 and p. 48; "Experiment in Criticism," p. 201 and p. 208; *After Strange Gods* (N. Y.: Harcourt, Brace & Co., 1934), p. 34.

[22] *Use of Poetry,* p. 65. Cf. "Experiment in Criticism," p. 200ff.

[23] *Ibid.,* p. 87.

[24] *Ibid.,* p. 88. These statements are somewhat oversimplified. What is in the Romantics generically is like what is in much neo-classical criticism. The Romantics inherited much of the neo-classical predisposition to make literature the handmaid of morality.

step be necessary," Eliot concludes, "to finding in literature the satisfaction which we deny ourselves in religion."[25]

Modern criticism, Eliot thinks, is still demanding from poetry the values which Arnold sought, though now the confusion is expressed

> in several forms. I find it in the humanism of Irving Babbitt, and in the more recent theories of critics of such opposed views as Middleton Murry and I. A. Richards. Mr. Murry seems to maintain that poetry is religion; Mr. Richards rather more moderately that poetry is the best thing we can have nowadays instead of religion.[26]

This confusion Eliot finds disturbing because it may "distort our enjoyment of poetry."[27] By looking to poetry for religion and emphasizing that aspect of it, "the judgment of poetry as poetry will become of dwindling interest."

Another substitution which Eliot has inveighed against is the

---

[25] *John Dryden* (1932), p. 65. This same idea appears also in "Arnold and Pater," *Sel. Essays,* p. 396. The necessity for intellectuality in religion Eliot stated in a review of Baron von Hügel's *Selected Letters* which appeared in *The Dial,* LXXXIV (1928), 112: "We demand of religion some kind of intellectual satisfaction—both private and local—or we do not want it at all."

[26] *John Dryden* (1932), p. 66. Cf. also "The Modern Mind," *Use of Poetry,* pp. 121-142.

[27] See also "Second Thoughts About Humanism," *Sel. Essays,* p. 448, in which Eliot states that "this trick of making literature do the work of philosophy, ethics, and theology, tends to vitiate one's judgment and sensibility in literature. . . ." In connection with this subject, one can note another of those near-parallelisms to Remy de Gourmont in the essay on "Matthew Arnold" in *The Use of Poetry,* p. 112: "The greatness of a poet," Eliot quotes Arnold as saying, "lies in his powerful and beautiful application of ideas to life." As Arnold uses the word *ideas* he means moral ideas as can be discerned from the context. Eliot comments: "Not a happy way of putting it, as if ideas were a lotion for the inflamed skin of suffering humanity." Speaking of the futility of seeking morality from art, Remy de Gourmont wrote in *La Culture des Idées,* p. 106: "Admettre l'art parce qu'il peut moraliser les individus ou les masses, c'est admettre les roses parce qu'on en tire un remède utile aux yeux."

misuse of poetry which seeks philosophic systems from it.[28] Dante
and Shakespeare both used philosophies which were at hand.
That Dante had an Aquinas behind him and Shakespeare had the
inferior philosophy of Seneca in no way vitiates the poetry of
Shakespeare.[29] It does not make Dante a greater poet, or mean
that we learn more from Dante than from Shakespeare.[30] When
philosophy is incorporated into poetry, it ceases to function primarily as philosophy and becomes "the philosophy of that world
of poetry which we have entered."[31]

The great error of substitution has always overshadowed poetry
because of the material of which it is made—words—though the
modern forms of the heresy appear more futile than the ancient
ones of the same variety. One may conclude from Eliot's criticism
that he considers that Wordsworth, Shelley, and Arnold have so
mistaken the nature of poetry that they have not kept the primary
purpose of writing it in mind. Because they have been mistaken
in their use of the means for reaching the end they had in mind,
they have achieved neither great poetry nor the goal for which
they wrote. The presented factors which are constituents of poetry
are ordered, but not in the effort to persuade men to action in

---

[28] See "William Blake," *Sel. Essays,* p. 322; "Dante," *Sac. Wood;* "Shakespeare and Stoicism of Seneca, *Sel. Essays;* "Seneca in Elizabethan Translation" (1927); the "Introduction" to *The Wheel of Fire* (1930); "Poetry
and Propaganda," *The Bookman* (1930), 601; and the various essays on
Donne. In "Literature and the Modern World," *American Prefaces,* I
(1935), 20, Eliot treated the problem of the relation of poetry and social
ideals. His solution to this was "what is desirable is a harmony between
the individual and sub-individual passions of the artist, and the social ideas
and feelings which he wishes to propagate. In this harmony, he neither
exploits the conscious doctrine as a vehicle for his personality nor cramps
or distorts his personality to adapt it to a social doctrine. . . ."

[29] *Sel. Essays,* p. 96.

[30] *Ibid.,* p. 135.

[31] Miss Dorothy Walsh has stated this position most happily: "The fact is
that natural piety toward the experientially given, whether it be a theoretical
conception, a human experience, or a material object, is foreign to the artist,
who is not a reporter but a creator. Anything that God or nature, philosophy
or science, politics or history, or art itself, can give him is not going to
be accepted as something finished and as such to be respected. It is going to
be reduced to the level of raw material for a new creation." "The Cognitive
Content of Art," *The Philosophical Review,* LII (1943), 436.

the moral sphere, nor for the presentation of a system of factual knowledge. All of Eliot's early criticism had as its central problem "the integrity of poetry,"[32] and he has continued to reiterate that "poetry cannot prove that anything is true."[33] Poetry is only concerned with showing that "certain worlds of thought and feeling are possible."[34]

---

[32] *Sac. Wood,* p. viii.

[33] Cf. *The Bookman* (1930), 601: "For poetry . . . is not the assertion that something is true, but the making that truth more fully real to us; it is the creation of a sensuous embodiment." That "poetic truth" is different from logical truth for Eliot may be seen from the review of the letters of J. B. Yeats which Eliot published in *The Egoist,* IV (1917), 90. After quoting Mr. Yeats who said "the poet does not seek to be original, but the truth," [*sic*] he comments: "Mr. Yeats understands poetry better than anyone I have ever known who was not a poet, and better than most of those who have the reputation of poets. This last quotation, in fact, is a thought which takes very deep roots; it strikes through the tangle of literature direct to the subsoil of the greatest—to Shakespeare and Dante and Aeschylus. Ordinary writers of verse either deal in imagination or in 'ideas'; they escape from one to the other, but neither one nor the other nor both together is truth in the sense of 'poetic truth.'"

[34] *The Bookman* (1930), 602. Cf. also *Sel. Essays,* p. 259. The mention of *possible* awakens echoes of Aristotle who had said in the *Poetics*: " . . . it will be seen that the poet's function is to describe, not the thing that has happened, but a kind of thing that might happen, *i.e.* what is possible as being probable or necessary. . . . Hence poetry is something more philosophic and of graver import than history, since its statements are of the nature rather of universals, whereas those of history are singulars." (1451a36-1451b6, Bywater's trans.) How possibility aspires to the condition of universality Eliot describes in the following passage, *The Criterion,* XII (1932-33), 248: "There are also people who, while recognizing the interest of the work of literature as a document upon the ideas and the sensibility of its epoch, and recognizing even that the permanent work of literature is one which does not lack this interest, yet cannot help valuing literary work, like philosophical work, in the end by its transcendence of the limits of its age; by its breaking through the categories of thought and sensibility of its age; by its speaking, in the language of its time and in the imagery of its own tradition, the word which belongs to no time. Art, we feel, aspires to the condition of the timeless. . . ." Philosophy deals with statements which aspire to present universal truths. One of the principal pleasures which can be derived from philosophy is the pleasure which comes from any effort toward unification. Poetry, because it is concerned neither with particular nor general truths (since it deals with possibility), aspires to a different unity. Whatever claims

If one is to realize completely Eliot's concept of the function of meaning in poetry, the key to understanding is in interpreting the phrase "of thought and feeling" not as two distinct activities but as cognitive and emotional stimuli constantly interacting and affecting each other. "The poet who 'thinks,'" he wrote in 1927, "is merely the poet who can express the emotional equivalent of thought."[35] So in the completed poetical product cognitional references have an equivalent in emotional stimuli. For a poet to transpose into poetry the "value of the thought current at [his] time,"[36] is for him to transfer into the poetic object references which will express not just cognitions but corresponding and accompanying affectiveness. The final cause of poetry then, as Eliot conceives it, must also be closely connected with this affective expression; and in 1927 he stated quite unmistakably that the "function [of poetry] is not intellectual but emotional."[37] The ultimate result is to create a unity of feeling. It is significant that Eliot mentioned this same result in discussing the Elizabethan drama. Both the unity of place and the unity of time may be violated, he asserted, "if we observe more closely the law of Unity of Sentiment."[38]

The relation of efficient cause to final cause, or the process of poetry which Eliot has described here, is similar to that of expressionistic aesthetic as it emerged from the nineteenth century, in which a process of expression identified ontologically the expressive matter with the *exprimends* in the mind of the *expressor*.[38a] In his description of the process, Eliot has modified this theory

---

poetry has to universality are linked always with the unity of the artistic order. Recent commentary upon the possible has been furnished by Miss D. Walsh in *The Philosophical Review*, LII, 445, where she outlines the main thesis of her argument: "The possible, as it relates to a conceptual context, may be called ideal possibility. I suggest that such ideal possibility may be classified as follows: (1) the formally possible, as for example, in pure mathematics; (2) the hypothetical, as for example, in scientific theory—this is the statement of what is probably actual; (3) the alternative, presented as I believe in art—this is an internally coherent or compossible scheme presented as alternative to the actual."

[35] *Sel. Essays,* p. 134.

[36] *Ibid.,* p. 136.

[37] *Ibid.,* p. 138. This is corroborated in the *Clark Lectures.*

[38] *Use of Poetry,* p. 36.

[38a] On these terms, see Shipley's *Dictionary,* art. "Expression," pp. 225-227.

somewhat. The emotions and feelings which function in poetry are not for him identified exclusively with the agent. If they are not severed completely from his psychological reactions, they are at least only ascribed to him as to an instrumental cause. It is well to note this modification, for we shall have occasion to discuss its implications later.

The presence of an affective stimulus helps us to discern when poetry occurs in prose if we are to judge by several statements which Eliot makes: "Is 'Absalom and Achitophel,' is the 'Letter to Arbuthnot,' poetry?" he challenged. "These are great literature; and I cannot see that it matters much whether we call them poetry or prose. In any case, they do something that great poetry does: they capture and put into literature an emotion."[39] That some prose may perform this function of capturing emotions Eliot acknowledged when he wrote that

> Launcelot Andrewes is, I think, a great prose writer, but you cannot really get at the poetry in his prose unless you are willing to read at least one of his sermons entire; his style preserves the content, yes, but you cannot get the pleasure of the style unless you interest yourself in something more than the words.[40]

Eliot's insistence upon the necessity of reading the work as a whole is a protest against trying to find the prose-poem in the "purple patch," the too frequent appearance of which he thinks disfigures the work of Sir Thomas Browne. In Andrewes the poetry is somewhat diffused throughout the entire structure and can only be apprehended after the whole structure of one of his sermons is read. On the other hand, the affective stimulus in the writings of Sir Thomas Browne and Jeremy Taylor does not sufficiently penetrate the structure. Therefore, there is nothing in their work that is worth "preserving." Eliot charges that they are mediocre "of mind," "diffuse," and "precisely lacking in that intensity which raises the history of Newman's religious doubts

---

[39] *The Chapbook,* No. 22 (1921), 7.
[40] *Ibid.,* p. 7.

to the highest importance. . . ."[41] After analyzing a passage of
Browne's, Eliot concludes that though he recognizes certain felici-
ties of the sound structure, he is forced to affirm that the passage
is but "a pinch of dust, and therefore there is not really great
style." The Grave Digger Scene in *Hamlet* (also written in prose),
certain poems of Donne, or Bishop King's "Exequy" for his dead
wife, are all great poetry because "in each of these a human
emotion is concentrated and fixed," but "in the prose of Sir Thomas
Browne only a commonplace sententiousness is decorated by rever-
berating language."

Ultimately, then, for either prose or verse to be called poetry,
a human emotion must be "fixed." But simply fixing an emotion
is not enough. The emotion must be "fixed" with *intensity* as
Eliot clearly states when he speaks of Newman. The relation of
this quality of intensity to the rest of Eliot's theory is an important one and its position will be indicated as this study proceeds.
But intensity need not be continuously present. In the *Chapbook*
essay, Eliot suggested what he jestingly called "the proper form"
of poetry. This would be a combination of "verse and prose in
waves of intense or relaxed feeling."[42]

Because a "single work must have some metrical unity," he
refuses to take this suggestion too seriously. But he is quite in
earnest when he comments that he is not committing himself to
the statement "that intensity of feeling should be expressed in
verse, or that verse should always be intense." If "the proper
form" of poetry may be a combination of prose and verse in
waves of intense and relaxed feeling, then once again we have a
text which points to the fact that the *differentia* of poetry is connected intimately with an affective stimulus. Furthermore, since
this affectivity "need not always be in verse, nor need verse
always be intense," poetry may be in either prose or verse structure. Since from the above investigation so much is clear, the
next problem is how this affectivity may be discerned in discourse. Three areas invite further inquiry: the matter of poetry,

---

[41] *Ibid.*, p. 7. Cf. what Eliot says of Andrewes' style in *Sel. Essays*, p. 334:
"The most conspicuous qualities of the style are three: ordonnance, or arrangement and structure, precision in the use of words, and relevant intensity."
[42] *Ibid.*, p. 5.

the way in which cognitive meanings are connected with affective meanings, and the manner in which affective meanings are brought into poetry.

II

The purpose of this section is to investigate the first subject noted above, the matter of poetry, to see if, for Eliot, there is any appreciable difference in the use of words in poetry and prose.

When Eliot wrote in the essay on *Ezra Pound,* "words are perhaps the hardest of all material of art," he certainly recognized that words have meanings; that in the phraseology of Ezra Pound they are "human symbols, conventions," which carry cognitions.[43]

On the other hand, as we have seen from preceding sections, Eliot's preoccupation with emotion and his shifting terminology make it difficult to affix one signification to any one term with precision. It has been noted earlier, for instance, that he repudiated the idea that verbal sound alone could be beautiful. Does he then consider that the poet should be primarily concerned with the cognitive meaning of words? In the preceding chapter, the deep interlocking of prose and poetry was apparent. It is but reasonable, consequently, to enquire, in speaking of meaning, whether there is any differentiating element in the significance of words which distinguishes prose from poetry.

That in 1921 Eliot described the condition of English literature as "lifeless" and asserted that any enquiry that should "stimulate the worn nerves and release the arthritic limbs of our diction," would be welcome, is sufficient to show that he was interested enough to speculate upon problems of language. He repudiated in that same year any distinction between prose and poetry which states that poetry is the "language of emotion and imagination— proceeding by concrete images—and . . . prose is the language of thought and ratiocination—proceeding by argument, by definition, by inference, by the use of abstract terms."[44] In short, for Eliot language as an element is not enough to distinguish between poetry and prose. Just as beautiful sound alone cannot produce poetry

---

[43] Ezra Pound, "George Antheil," *The Criterion,* II, 325.
[44] The *Chapbook,* No. 22 (1921), 8.

neither can figurative language, which refers to emotion, nor abstract language, which presents thought, be sufficient. That Eliot is, nevertheless, very much concerned with language, one who has read him widely could never doubt.

Several times Eliot quotes with relish Ezra Pound's dictum that verse as well as prose should be well written.[45] "Well written" may apply to the grammatical excellence of the sentence structure, but it may also resolve itself into a problem of diction. Attention has been called in the preceding section to the relationship between prose and verse, how one may contribute to the support of the other.[46] In several places Eliot advised both poets and critics to give their days and nights to a study not of Addison but of Jespersen.[47] But, though prose and poetry may have similar grammatical structure and though "the interaction between prose and verse . . . is a condition of vitality in literature," as discourses they have different functions, as we have seen. If the poetic function is not unmistakably necessary to a work, Eliot urges that prose be used, since "anything that can be said as well in prose can

---

[45] *Marianne Moore* (1935), p. 7; "Johnson's 'London,'" *passim*. On the general condition in both England and America Eliot commented as follows in his "London Letter" to *The Dial*, LXXII (1922), 512: "The English language is of course badly written in both countries. In England, it is not ungrammatical, but common; it is not in bad taste, but rather tasteless."

[46] See *John Dryden* (1932), pp. 10, 13, 43.

[47] In "Experiment in Criticism" and *The Music of Poetry* Eliot called attention to Jespersen's *English Grammar* which he had reviewed in *The New Criterion*, V (1927), 121-124. In an early essay, "A Brief Treatise on the Criticism of Poetry," *The Chapbook*, II, No. 9 (Mar., 1920), 4 he noted that poets can learn as much from Jespersen as from reading Sainte-Beuve. And his comment upon the *Memorandum for the Teaching of English* (*The Monthly Criterion*, VI, 1927, 291) is enlightening in several respects: "The Memorandum encourages the study of grammar (though one is surprised that it should have been thought necessary to defend that study). But it does not encourage the study of grammar after the age of thirteen. This is regrettable. Grammar should be made to lead up to the study of logic, modern logic, not the antiquated discipline of Barbara. Young people who continue the study of English after they are fifteen or sixteen, ought to learn how the language has been formed, ought to learn something of both historical and comparative grammar, and come to understand how much the work of logicians has done to make of English a language in which it is possible to think clearly and exactly on any subject."

be said better in prose."[48] Yet, grammatically, "English imposes less upon the writer than French." For variation, therefore, more demand is laid upon diction; "every word must be charged afresh with energy every time it is used; the language demands an animosity."[49] Determining what psychological functions words have for Eliot, then, resolves itself into a study of what he says about words themselves.

Dante's modest statement that his reason for writing the *De Vulgari Eloquentia* was "to be of service to the vernacular speech," might well preface many of Eliot's essays from the old *Egoist* days to the recent *What Is a Classic?* The focus of his emphasis has been the same: the duty of the poet to contribute to the language. How then may the poet do this? Because "literature must be judged by language," it is the duty of the poet "to develop the language."[50] "To the extent to which he is read"[51] the poet "is contributing toward the organic development of culture,"[52] and in so far as he neglects to contribute to this development, he becomes an agent of deterioration.[53] This responsibility of the

---

[48] *Use of Poetry,* p. 152.

[49] "London Letter," *The Dial,* LXXII (1922), 512.

[50] "Disjecta Membra," *The Egoist,* V, 55.

[51] "Observations," *The Egoist,* V, 69.

[52] "Contemporanea," *The Egoist,* V, 84. Cf. also a review in *The New Criterion,* V (1927), 122: "To preserve a language from death is the first duty of those who speak it." Also "The Minor Metaphysicals," *The Listener,* III (Apr. 9, 1930), 641: "Our language, or any civilized language, is like the phoenix; it springs anew from its own ashes. And correct language *is* civilization."

[53] The notion of the poet's contribution to the language has, of course, an ancient pedigree. Aristotle gave special attention to the language of the poet both in the *Poetics* and the *Rhetoric.* Horace devoted twenty-five precious lines to a discussion of it. Dante's purpose has already been noted. (But see Vernon Hall's *Renaissance Literary Criticism,* pp. 18-19 for what he concludes Dante meant by "vernacular speech.") Dryden in the "Dedication" of the *Aeneis* proclaimed that he traded "both with the living and the dead, for the enrichment of our native language." And Coleridge echoes Dante in the *Biographia Literaria*: "I should plead inwardly guilty to the charge of duplicity or cowardice, if I withheld my conviction, that few have guarded the purity of their native tongue with that jealous care, which the sublime Dante in his tract 'De la nobile volgare eloquenza' declares to be the first duty of a poet. For language is the armoury of the human kind; and at once

poet Eliot called "permanent" in a broadcast during 1944 where he reiterated the obligation of the poet to be alive to what is being done elsewhere:

> But we should know, after the mutual isolation of these five years, that no one language, and no one literature of Europe, can maintain itself in full health and vigor when cut off from communication with the others. Thus our several responsibilities are related to a common responsibility.[54]

By his awareness of what is happening in his art, not only in his own country, but also in the literature of those ethnic groups which constitute the cultural unit to which he belongs, the poet is affecting a process which Eliot denominated "fertilization."[55] But as preparation for his contribution to its vitality, the poet must study ceaselessly and untiringly "how his language has been written, in both prose and verse, in the past,"[56] and he must exhibit

---

contains the trophies of its past, and the weapons of its future conquests" (Shawcross, II, p. 22). T. E. Hulme in one of his fragments noted: "Poetry is always the advance guard in language. The progress of language is the absorption of new analogies" (*The Criterion,* III, 490).

[54] Taken from a broadcast over BBC, Oct. 24, 1944. This is in the unpublished papers in the Henry Ware Eliot Collection of Eliotiana in the Houghton Library at Harvard University.

[55] "Commentary," *The Criterion,* XIV (1934-35), 611. For other developments of this idea, see *The Egoist,* V, 84; and *The Classics and the Man of Letters* (N. Y.: Oxford University Press, 1942).

[56] This has been the main burden of Ezra Pound's belligerent essays. See *The A B C of Reading; Culture; Polite Essays;* and *Make It New.* Eliot always takes for granted that the poet is a man of unusual intellectual development. "The possible interests of a poet are unlimited; the more intelligent he is the better; the more intelligent he is the more likely that he will have interests: our only condition is that he turn them into poetry, and not merely meditate on them poetically." *Sel. Essays,* p. 288. This idea reappeared in *The Classics and the Man of Letters,* p. 20: "Everything may be grist to his mill, and the more knowledge of every kind that he can assimilate the better; the serious distinction for him, is between the subjects which he should be taught, and the subjects which he should acquire by himself." But the poet must beware of confusing certain types of training: ". . . there is a philosophic training, and it is not the literary training; there are rules of the philosophic game about the use and definition of terms, and they are not the literary rules." *Sel. Essays,* p. 488. There are also two

"sensitiveness to the merits and shortcomings of the way in which it is spoken and written in his own time."[57] "What he can do with his language" is the problem which arises afresh in every generation and is the one of which the poet "can afford to be most conscious." His point of departure must be "the language as it is spoken in his own time."[58] Because "a language is always changing, its developments in vocabulary, in syntax, pronunciation and intonation—even in the long run—its deterioration—must be accepted by the poet and made the best of."[59]

---

other notes on the poets' education which are worth recording. The first is in the 1920 essay on Blake (*Ibid.*, p. 319). Here Eliot observes that the poet needs to be highly educated in his own art; but the actual information acquired in ordinary education is apt to impose a conformity which is harmful to the poet in obscuring "what we really are and feel, what we really want, and what really excites our interest." The second, in "The Mysticism of Blake," *The Nation and Athenaeum* (1927), 779, asserted that education meant not only erudition "but a kind of mental and moral discipline. The great poet—even the greatest—knows his own limitations and works within them. . . . The poet also knows that it is no good, in writing poetry, to try to be anything but a poet."

[57] *The New English Weekly*, XV (1939), 28. Eliot's idea of the function of criticism is closely bound up with the contribution of the poet to the vitality of the language. In 1918 he noted that "literature must be judged by language" ("Disjecta Membra," *The Egoist*, V, 55). Again in 1933 he wrote: "I hold indeed that in an age in which the use of poetry is something agreed upon you are more likely to get that minute and scrupulous examination of felicity and blemish, line by line, which is conspicuously absent from the criticism of our time, a criticism which seems to demand of poetry, not that it shall be well written, but that it shall be 'representative of its age.'" *Use of Poetry*, p. 25. It was because literary critics had not preserved intact the integrity of their point of view—that is, demanding that literature be well-written,—but had confounded their relation to poetry with the uses which representatives of other cultural disciplines might make of it, that Eliot proposed his "experiment in criticism"; that is, a return to the criticism of poetry using the standards of those "masters who have been forgotten." The excellence of its writing is one of poetry's most important "uses" to society. If critics must have a utilitarian value, this is it; and it is likewise the criterion by which they may begin objective evaluation.

[58] *The New English Weekly*, XV, 27-28.

[59] *Mus. of Poetry*, pp. 26-27. Cf. *The New English Weekly*, XV, 28: "Even if the language is deteriorated, the poet must start from where he is, and not from a point at which he believes the language to have been superior." Blake in his earlier works also exhibits the "struggle . . . against the continuous deterioration of language." *Sel. Essays*, p. 319.

While "every language has its own resources and its own limitations . . . the conditions of a language and the conditions of the
history of the people who speak it,"[60] are factors which must be
taken into consideration in attempting to evaluate what can be
produced. To produce a classic, Eliot thinks, maturity and compre-
hensiveness are qualities which the language must possess. But
he also maintains that "a particular poet and lifetime of labor on
the part of that poet" are also needed.[61]

One cannot generalize from any of the evidence given so far
that diction in poetry is any different from that of prose for
Eliot. In fact, he calls attention to Dryden because it was he
"who for the first time, and so far as we are concerned, for all
time, established a normal English speech, and speech valid for
both verse and prose."[62] What distinguishes the speech which is
good from the speech which is bad in literature is the employment
of the particular rather than the general word. Effective language
is that "which is struggling to digest and express new objects,
new groups of objects, new feelings, new aspects."[63] As examples
of artists who are struggling to do this he mentions James Joyce
and the earlier Conrad. Thus it is impossible to say that any particular kind of language may be isolated as a *differentia* for poetry.
Furthermore, he implies in the essay on "John Dryden" (1922)
that the aura of suggestiveness which usually surrounds the diction of poetry need not be too pervasive since the diction of
Dryden, though it states immensely, is almost without connota-

---

[60] *What Is a Classic?* p. 9.

[61] *Ibid.,* p. 9.

[62] *John Dryden* (1932), p. 21. In this respect Eliot usually links Donne
with Dryden as in the following: "But in truth Dryden and Donne are both
highly natural; and the merit of both is to have established a natural conversational diction instead of a conventional one. Each effected a revolution
of the kind which has to occur from time to time, which will have to occur
again in nearly measurable time, if the English language is to retain its
vigour." *A Garland for John Donne,* pp. 13-14. Cf., too, Eliot's approval of
Wordsworth in *Use of Poetry,* p. 74: "Where he wrote 'my purpose was
to imitate, and as far as possible, to adopt the very language of men' he was
saying what no serious critic could disapprove."

[63] *Sel. Essays,* p. 327.

tions. Swinburne, on the other hand, by suggesting everything, denotes nothing.[64]

In one text Eliot is quite explicit upon the structural quality of the meanings of words. "Modernist" verse, he finds, possesses

> either an excess or a defect of technical attention. The former appears in an emphasis upon words rather than things, and the latter in an emphasis upon things and an indifference to words. In either case, the poem is formless, just as the most accomplished sonnet, if it is an attempt to express matter unsuitable for sonnet form, is formless.[65]

On the other hand, when he speaks of the work of poets in relation to diction, though a certain emphasis is allotted to the intellectual element in meaning, one dominant idea can be seen running through all his criticism, and it is this which forms the basis for many of his critical judgments. Eliot censures most of the unfavorable criticism levelled against Swinburne, for instance, as wide of the mark because "the material, the human feelings," against which it is directed do not exist in Swinburne's work. Since "language in a healthy state presents the object, is so close to the object that the two are identified," and the object is equated with "human feelings," this can only mean that a healthy language in poetry presents human feelings.[66]

In the development of the English language, "that perpetual slight juxtaposition" which alters language into new meanings is evidence, Eliot thinks, of "a very high development of the senses." This does not mean, as it ordinarily would in strict psychological terminology, that the senses of such poets as Chapman, Middleton, Webster, Tourneur, and Donne exhibited unusual receptivity of sense impressions, but that their work showed such an integration of sensation and intellect that "sensation became word and word was sensation."[67] Donne's great inventiveness is shown in hovering "in content between thought and feeling."[68]

---

[64] *Ibid.*, p. 315.
[65] *Marianne Moore* (1935), p. 11.
[66] *Sel. Essays*, p. 327.
[67] *Ibid.*, p. 209.
[68] "The Devotional Poets," *The Listener*, III, p. 552.

Chesterton is praised for not obstructing the "sensibility of the language," though he did nothing to develop it.[69] From these and other examples one can see again that "meaning" for Eliot connotes intellectual and affective associations. Though the former is more or less always implied, the latter is given far the more prominent notice. There are instances where Eliot sweepingly attributes the qualities found in the poetry to the speech of the whole people. In *The Use of Poetry,* there is a text which ascribes not one but three psychological effects to poetry as the highest development of a people's speech. "The poetry of a people takes its life from the people's speech and in turn gives life to it; and represents the highest point of consciousness, its greatest power and its most delicate sensibility."[70] Between the people's speech and poetry there is a mutual interchange.[71] The poet, accepting the raw material of the speech, develops and refines it in his works. In so far as he is a member of the group using this language, his contribution to it partakes of anonymity. But the attributes, consciousness, power, and sensibility, are psychological states or faculties. How can these terms be applied generally to such an inorganic

---

[69] *The Criterion,* XVI (1936-37), 69. Cf. *Sel. Essays,* p. 155: "Their words [Shakespeare, Donne, Tourneur, Middleton] have often a network of tentacular roots reaching down to the deepest terrors and desires." Wit, which Eliot calls in one place "reason, or even urbanity," is a "quality of sophisticated literature." But "when we come to Gray and Collins, the sophistication remains only in the language, but has disappeared from the feeling." *Sel. Essays,* p. 296. In the essay on "The Metaphysical Poets" he shows that while the language in some respects improved in the eighteenth century. "the feeling became more crude." "The feeling, the sensibility, expressed in the Country Churchyard . . . is cruder than that in the *Coy Mistress." Ibid.,* p. 288. To fail to express the moods of Baudelaire in English is not merely a failure of translation, but shows "an impotence to use words definitely" because one cannot feel the moods of Baudelaire. *Essays, Ancient & Modern,* p. 72. Byron's "schoolboy command of language" indicates a defective sensibility for practical purposes. "If the writer has not the language in which to express feelings they might as well not exist." *From Anne to Victoria,* p. 612. Shakespeare probably has done more than any poet "to make the English language capable of expressing the most subtle thought or the most refined shades of feeling." *What Is a Classic?* p. 12.

[70] *Use of Poetry,* p. 15. For other such generalizations, see *Sel. Essays,* p. 67 and *What Is a Classic?* p. 27.

[71] *Mus. of Poetry, passim.*

object as speech? Eliot seems to be ascribing to the abstract term, "people's speech," the psychological factors which were operative in the poets who produced the best poetry in that speech. This example of referring organic states to inorganic things is not an isolated instance. But one should also note that "consciousness" and "power" as attributes of speech imply cognition and capacity for such, and therefore, connote intellectual references.

It is in stressing intellectuality that Eliot says of comment upon Marianne Moore that her work "is utterly intellectual, but not abstract; the word never parts from the feeling; her ideas, imageless, remain quite personal."[72] Eliot notes that the intellectuality of Miss Moore's work can be recognized by the fact that she states her ideas directly instead of using figurative language. In his opinion what saves her words, which embody these imageless ideas, from becoming abstract is the cooperation of a personal feeling.[73]

In the prefatory essay to Miss Moore's poems, however, the relation of the poet to the language of poetry is stated unmistakably. It is the function of the living poet to carry out "that struggle for the maintenance of a living language, for the maintenance of its strength, its subtlety, for the preservation of the quality of feeling, which must be kept up in every generation."[74] Again Eliot wrote in 1939 that if the level of literacy amongst poets were to decrease, the future of the language and also the future of sensibility would be in jeopardy since "what we cease to try to find

---

[72] *The Egoist,* V (1918), 70.

[73] But in so far as any word is intelligible, is it not intellectual? Can we oppose intellectual and abstract in this way? *Intellectual* refers to a psychological process performed by the understanding, a process which is always one of abstraction whether the referent be abstract or concrete. *Abstract* points to or alludes to a quality in the referent. The meaning of every word, whether abstract or concrete, is intellectual, and both kinds may evoke affective reactions. The sphere of operational effect of affectivity is not confined to certain psychological areas but is co-active with all mental processes. Furthermore, if the words which Miss Moore uses to connote her meanings are individualized by feelings, how can these words tell us what *her* feelings are? She may use such combinations to evoke certain effects for her readers, but how can one ever know through the poetic object what the author's personal emotions are?

[74] *Marianne Moore* (1935), p. 6.

words for we cease to be able to feel."[75] So the vitality which the poet seeks to preserve is a vitality in the "quality of feeling." This is merely another way of saying what had been asserted in the essay on Philip Massinger in 1920 that "every vital development in language is a development of feeling as well."[76] The poet is greatly concerned with language and Eliot imposes upon him the duty of preserving the quality of it. It is not the subtlety with which language might assert cognitional effects, however, but the quality of affectivity which it vitalizes that makes the poet's use important.

This investigation of the matter of poetry has merely emphasized what is becoming increasingly clearer; *viz.,* the identification of the *differentia* of poetry with some form of affective expression. But Eliot describes no distinguishing quality in the language that would set it apart for poetry. Language as language will not supply a *differentia* and it is not reference to a certain set of objects or ideas that characterizes poetry for Eliot. He recognizes, in other words, no diction as specifically poetic. It is only when language has been given a definite structure that it becomes poetry. And then the "secondary meanings" become as important as the cognitive denotations. To see how the quality of feeling is allied to cognitive meanings in the total structure, then, must be the next task.

III

If the final cause of poetry for Eliot is to capture an emotion and if the function of the poet in using his material is to preserve quality of feeling, how does this affect the formal structure of poetry? Is there a special character to the meaning of poetry? In short, what is poetic meaning? The importance of this problem is eminently apparent in the fact that from time to time Eliot finds it necessary to stress the ontological objectivity of poetry.

> The poem's existence is somewhere between the writer and the reader; it has a reality which is not simply the

---

[75] *The New English Weekly,* XV, 28.
[76] *Sel. Essays,* p. 210.

reality of what the writer is trying to "express," or of his experiences writing it, or of the experience of the reader or of the writer as reader. Consequently the problem of what a poem "means" is a good deal more difficult than it at first appears.[77]

"Thought" or reference to logical propositions is usually referred to as *meaning* in modern criticism, and that is what Eliot seems to have in mind by the word when he discusses it in *The Use of Poetry*:

> The chief use of the "meaning" of a poem, in the ordinary sense, may be . . . to satisfy one habit of the reader, to keep his mind diverted and quiet, while the poem does its work upon him. . . . This is a normal situation of which I approve. But the minds of all poets do not work that way; some of them, assuming that there are other minds like their own, become impatient of this "meaning" which seems superfluous, and perceive possibilities of intensity through its elimination.[78]

Though others might try to eliminate meaning, Eliot accepts the presence of it as a "normal situation." Because of the very nature of words, conceptual references must be present, even though "a great deal, in the way of meaning, belongs to prose rather than to poetry."[79]

But since poetry does use words and since the mind does operate as a unit and intellection is one of the phases of this operation, how are thought and feeling compossible to Eliot? One need not infer

---

[77] *Use of Poetry*, p. 30. Cf. a like description in the 1928 preface to *The Sacred Wood*, p. x: "We can only say that a poem, in some sense, has its own life; that its parts form something quite different from a body of neatly ordered biographical data; that the feeling, or emotion, or vision, resulting from the poem is something different from the feeling or emotion or vision in the mind of the poet."

[78] *Use of Poetry*, p. 151. For another such use of *meaning* in modern criticism, cf. Hopkins' *Notebooks and Papers* (*The Criterion*, XV, 11): "Some matter and meaning is essential to it [poetry] but only as an element necessary to support and employ the shape which is contemplated for its own sake."

[79] *Use of Poetry*, p. 152.

that a poem is built on an "idea."[80] But it does mean that because poems are built of words and words have meanings which give concepts as well as percepts, the poem must be a structure of meanings.

It is this latter interpretation which Eliot seemed to support in an earlier discussion of this subject:

> . . . people ordinarily incline to suppose that in order to enjoy a poem it is necessary to "discover its meaning" so that their minds toil to discover a meaning, a meaning which they can expound to any one who will listen, in order to prove that they enjoy it. But for one thing the possibilities of "meaning" in poetry are so extensive, that one is quite aware that one's knowledge of the meaning even of what oneself has written is extremely limited, and that its meaning to others, at least so far as there is some consensus of interpretation among persons apparently qualified to interpret, is quite as much a part of it as what it means to oneself.[81]

That "the possibilities of 'meaning' in poetry are . . . extensive," cannot be over-emphasized. As Eliot has stated many times, poetry is not to supply information. It is not its business to present truths that are immediately recognizable. On the other hand, the unity of each individual poem is unique in its complex of references.

---

[80] Cf. "Introduction" to the *Collected Poems of Harold Monro,* p. xiii: "It is a poet's business to be original, in all that is comprehended by 'technique,' dictated, not by the idea—for there is no idea—but by the nature of that dark embryo within him which gradually takes on the form and speech of a poem."

[81] "Introduction," *Wheel of Fire,* pp. xiv-xv. The limitations of the poet with his own work Eliot has described in more detail in *The Use of Poetry,* p. 130: "A poet can try, of course, to give an honest report of the way in which he himself writes; the result may, if he is a good observer, be illuminating. And in one sense, but a very limited one, he knows better what his poems 'mean' than can any one else: he may know the history of their composition, the material which has gone in and come out in an unrecognizable form, and he knows what he was trying to do and what he was meaning to mean. But what a poem means is as much what it means to others as what it means to the author; and indeed, in the course of time a poet may become merely a reader in respect to his own works, forgetting his original meaning—or without forgetting, merely changing."

In the *Music of Poetry,* Eliot explained this expansion of possibilities of meaning by the fact that the "poet is occupied with frontiers of consciousness beyond which words fail, though meanings still exist." The phrase, "frontiers of consciousness,"[82] recalls the "frontiers of the spirit" which the poet is constantly exploring.[83] Thus the poetry that Eliot is alluding to would seem to be the work which has been the outgrowth of the Symbolists, although his generalization is just as valid for any other kind. Eliot's theory here suggests another area that oscillates "between fixity and flux." He has described this modern poetry elsewhere as "something distilled."[84] But the expansion of meanings of this poetry is usually in inverse ratio to the "distillation," since connotative diction usually replaces denotative. However, "frontiers of consciousness" and "frontiers of the spirit" are terms that suggest a vague, esoteric process which does not mingle well with classical clarity; and Eliot has given two matter-of-fact explanations in *The Music of Poetry* which explain this phenomenon of meaning unmistakably:

> A poem may appear to mean very different things to different readers, and all of these meanings may be different from what the author thought he meant. For instance, the author may have been writing some peculiar personal experience, which he saw quite unrelated to anything outside; yet for the reader the poem may become the expression of a general situation, as well as of some private experience of his own. The reader's interpretation may differ from the author's and be equally valid—it may even be better. There may be much more in a poem than the

---

[82] *Music of Poetry,* p. 15.

[83] *The New English Weekly,* XV, 27. This phrase likewise suggests Valéry's frequent use of such terms.

[84] "Byron," *From Anne to Victoria,* p. 602: "We have come to expect poetry to be something very concentrated, something distilled." Cf. Ker's *Form and Style* where Pindar's Fourth Pythian Ode is likened to a poem by Gautier. Ker comments that one cannot say that "this old Greek was tired of epic length, for epic was not his business, but he has, if not a dislike of plain narrative, yet a desire for the other kind of thing, for the poetry that distils, that gets the essence, sacrificing everything to feeling, here the feeling of anticipation, of mingled hope and dread" (Pp. 289-290).

author was aware of. The different interpretations may all be partial formulations of one thing; the ambiguities may be due to the fact that the poem means more, not less, than ordinary speech can communicate.[85]

Each person who reads a poem tends to generalize. Since the poem is a structure of particulars, these generalizations may be different, yet each may be equally valid. On the other hand, a poem is not just a structure of meanings. As we have seen in Chapter Two, it is likewise a structure of sounds whose fitness contributes materially to the unity of the whole work.[86]

Recognizing the possibility that the total meaning structure cannot be completely described in cognitive terms, Eliot wrote in his conclusion of his discussion of meaning in *The Wheel of Fire*: ". . . the sceptical practitioner of verse tends to limit his criticism of poetry to the appreciation of vocabulary and syntax, the analysis of line, metric and cadence; to stick as closely to the more trustworthy senses as possible."[87] And as one reads, at times one wishes that Eliot had been a little more sceptical in his criticism. But his recognition that the sound structure is just as important as meaning—that it suggests a kind of meaning of its own—is another contribution for which English criticism of the twentieth century is indebted to him.

Since, however, Eliot has said that he thinks that providing congenial meaning is a "normal situation," how does he suggest that this should be done?

In the *Clark Lectures* he describes three ways in which thought may be fused into poetry. Although the first two types are interesting and would provide material for stimulating discussion, it is by concentrating upon the third type of which he speaks that Eliot's conception of poetry can best be understood. This is metaphysical poetry of which he has written so much, and Mario Praz has given Eliot's definition from the *Clark Lectures* in his essay, "Donne and the Poetry of His Time": "I take as metaphysical poetry that in which what is ordinarily apprehensible only

---

[85] *The Music of Poetry*, pp. 15-16.
[86] *Ibid.*, p. 28 and *Use of Poetry*, pp. 144-145.
[87] *The Wheel of Fire*, p. xv.

by thought is brought within the grasp of feeling, or that in which what is ordinarily only felt is transformed into thought without ceasing to be feeling."[88] This is the type of *wit* poetry which Eliot thinks is most deserving of the name of poetry; because " 'wit' stands for a kind of balance and proportion of intellectual and emotional values."[89] It is about this last class that Eliot has written the most and to which he has devoted most of his critical attention. Therefore, it is by examining what he says here, that the clearest understanding is obtainable of the relationships of meaning to form in poetry.

As Eliot maintained in "The Metaphysical Poets," for Donne "a thought . . . was an experience; it modified his sensibility." Cognitions in other words effect and determine emotional reactions. The philosopher, Eliot wrote in the early essay on Dante, is trying to "realize" ideas and this effort is not the effort which the poet puts forth. The poet's use of philosophy is not for the presentation of an argument to support the truth of an assertion, but to use it as a datum of perception "when it has become almost a physical modification."[90] Or, as Eliot tersely stated it toward the end of this essay: "Dante, more than any other poet, has succeeded in dealing with his philosophy, not as a theory—or as his own comment or reflection, but in terms of something *perceived*."[91]

---

[88] Mario Praz, "Donne and the Poetry of His Time," *A Garland for John Donne, 1631-1931*, ed. T. Spencer (Cambridge: Harvard University Press, 1931), p. 58. Cf. W. T. Stace's idea of beauty: ". . . beauty is the fusion of an intellectual content, consisting of empirical non-perceptual concepts, with a perceptual field, in such manner that the intellectual content and the perceptual field are indistinguishable from one another; and in such manner as to constitute the revelation of an aspect of reality." *The Meaning of Beauty* (London: Grant Richards and Humphrey Toulmin, 1929), p. 43.

[89] "Notes on Two Odes of Cowley," *Studies in Honor of Sir H. J. C. Grierson* (Oxford: Clarendon Press, 1938), p. 242. Cf. the various essays on Donne.

[90] *Sac. Wood*, p. 163.

[91] *Ibid.*, pp. 170-171. There are many texts throughout the *Clark Lectures* which corroborate this statement. See also "Rhyme and Reason," *The Listener*, III (Mar., 1930), p. 503: ". . . this borderland where an emotion turns into a thought and a thought turns into an emotion is Donne's special province." *The Bookman*, LXX (1930), 601: "In reading Lucretius or Dante" what we find is "that the poet has effected a fusion between that

If we probe this in the light of some of his other statements, probably no other text yields so much to the understanding of Eliot's concept as this one. When Eliot underlines the word *perceived* as he has done in this context, one may look for the special meaning which he wishes to emphasize. In this instance it is a reference to the opening phrases of the *Posterior Analytics,* which in Eliot's interpretation state that "not only all knowledge, but all feeling, is in perception."[92] Therefore, when Eliot says that "Dante deals with his philosophy in terms of something perceived," he implies several alternatives: either that Dante uses the various parts of his material only in the perceptive state; *i.e.,* not as intellectual cognitions but as sensory impressions; or, that the poetic object into which he has woven his philosophy is apprehended by the receptor in its aesthetic completeness not as an abstraction but as a synthesis of sensory impressions and conceptual references; or that the philosophy is translated into terms of something else, something which it is possible to perceive, and that this equivalent object is not only a sensory stimulus but an affective stimulus as well. It is in the last sense that Eliot uses the word *perceived.* He implies that the important part of the act of perceiving for poetry is not the unifying of sensory impressions on a sub-intellectual level but is rather the act of being aware of the accompanying emotions. *This* is the element he wishes to stress. In the early essay on Dante he wrote: "The poem has not a framework, but a form; and even if the framework be allegorical, the form may be something else. The examination of any episode in the *Comedy* ought to show that not merely allegorical interpretation or the didactic intention, but the emotional significance itself, cannot be isolated from the rest of the poem."[93] What constitutes the form is the "emotional structure within this scaffold" and this structure

---

philosophy and his natural feelings, so that the philosophy becomes real, and the feelings become elevated, intensified and dignified." *A Garland for John Donne,* pp. 12-13: Donne's interest in the feel of an idea urges him "to arrest it, to play catlike with it, to develop it dialectically, to extract every minim of the emotion suspended in it."

[92] *Sac. Wood,* p. 10. Eliot has also made a reference to this work in *Sel. Essays,* p. 337.

[93] *Sac. Wood,* p. 165.

is "an ordered scale of human emotions,"[94] so that the whole work is, as he wrote later, "intellectual sanction for feeling, and esthetic sanction for thought."[95]

Poetry then consists of a unified pattern of sound structure and words which have two kinds of reference or meaning: intellectual and affective. Though he stresses the second kind to the apparent exclusion of the first, nevertheless, when one recalls that Eliot insists that the presence of an intellectual "meaning" is a "normal situation" in poetry, that he frowns upon the separation of prose and poetry on the basis that one uses a language of "emotion and imagination" and the other a language of "thought and ratiocination," and that he criticizes the poetry of Swinburne because of a deficiency of denotations, it is clear that Eliot always assumes the necessary cooperation between these two meanings. This reciprocal relationship of meanings joins with the sound structure to make the "music" of poetry. How the intellectual and affective meanings are related, Eliot has described in *A Choice of Kipling's Verse*:

> It is a question then of what one chooses to be conscious of, and of how much of the meaning, in a poem, is conveyed direct to the intelligence and how much is conveyed indirectly by the musical impression upon the sensibility —always remembering that the use of the word "musical" and of musical analogies, in discussing poetry, has its dangers if we do not constantly check its limitations: for the music of verse is inseparable from the meanings and associations of words.[96]

This emotional significance Eliot termed "secondary meaning" in *The Music of Poetry*: "My purpose here is to insist that a 'musical poem' is a poem which has a musical pattern of sound and a musical pattern of the secondary meanings of the words which compose it . . . and that these two patterns are indissoluble and one."[97] Just as the structure of sound forms a pattern, so too the affective meanings form what Eliot has termed "a musical

---

[94] *Ibid.*, p. 168.
[95] *The Bookman*, LXX (1930), 602.
[96] *A Choice of Kipling's Verse*, p. 18.
[97] *Mus. of Poetry*, p. 19.

pattern of the secondary meanings." It is this affective pattern which is the significant meaning for poetry as Eliot quite explicitly stated in this same address: "If we are moved by a poem, it has meant something, perhaps something important, to us; if we are not moved, then it is, as poetry, meaningless."[98]

All of these, the sound structure and the cognitive and affective meanings, are elements which become part of the form of poetry. And the affective meaning is as important as any other structural element. In the essay on Marianne Moore, Eliot remarked: "The first aspect in which Miss Moore's poetry is likely to strike the reader is that of minute detail rather than that of emotional unity."[99] Of Dryden Eliot maintained that neglect of him is not "due to the fact that his work is not poetry, but to a prejudice that the material, the feelings, out of which he built is not poetic."[100] The most elaborate presentation of this idea that the affective meaning is a formal element occurs in the essay entitled, "That Poetry Is Made With Words":

> It is true, I think, that poetry, if it is not to be a lifeless repetition of forms, must be constantly exploring "the frontiers of the spirit." But these frontiers are not like the surveys of geographical explorers, conquered once for all and settled. The frontiers of the spirit are more like the jungle which, unless continuously kept under control, is always ready to encroach and eventually obliterate the cultivated area. Our effort is as much to regain, under very different conditions, what was known to men writing at remote times and in alien languages. . . . But emotions themselves are constantly being lost; they can never be merely preserved, and must be always re-discovered; and it is as much this endless battle to regain civilization, in the midst of continuous outer and inner change of history, as the struggle to conquer the absolutely new, that is the occupation of the poet.[101]

[98] *Ibid.,* p. 15.
[99] *Marianne Moore* (1935), p. 7.
[100] *Sel. Essays,* p. 309.
[101] *The New English Weekly,* XV (1939), 27. Cf. Eliot's review of I. A. Richards' *Science and Poetry, The Dial,* LXXXII (1927), 243: "Mr. Richards is very well aware—as I know from conversations with him—and I know of no one who is more aware—that emotions and sentiments appear and disappear in the course of human history, and rapidly."

To prevent "a lifeless repetition of forms" the poet must be constantly alive to the affective meaning of his work. Not only by striving for the very new, but by resurrecting and revitalizing emotions which other poets in alien traditions have captured, may the poet prevent atrophy in the forms of poetry, so Eliot holds.

Meanings in poetry then are composed not only of cognitive references but also of affective ones. Other discourses may be concerned only with the first; the thought presented is the important element for them, but in poetry the affective meaning assumes first place. This affective meaning is not to be totally isolated from either the sound structure or the cognitive meaning structure, as the quotation from *A Choice of Kipling's Verse* on the "music" of poetry and the fact that he calls it a "secondary" meaning show. The total structure of poetry is an object which needs all of these elements for the perfecting of it. But as the sound structure cannot differentiate poetry, and as the abstract or purely factual communication of thought for didactic purposes is, inferentially, assigned to prose, the *differentia* of poetry must be somehow intimately related to this affective or secondary meaning.

The poet as a member of society is contributing to its good by using language so that it preserves quality of feeling. In his work he utilizes thought best by presenting it as something perceived: *i.e.,* as something in which the thought is felt. Meaning for him, then, has a two-fold import: it possesses not only intellectual but also affective structure. The latter supersedes the former in importance and becomes the significant meaning. Since it is the function of poetry either to "fix an emotion" or "to bring thought within the grasp of feeling," the next point of enquiry is: can the *differentia* of poetry be determined by the manner in which this affective meaning is presented in poetry?

IV

Those who have followed the general progress of Eliot's writings through the almost thirty years that he has been publishing criticism cannot but be struck by the variety of questions which he has grappled with and the deep consideration which he must have accorded them to have arrived at the solutions which he proffers. Consistency of position is hard to maintain in any sphere. In the field of literary criticism it is no easier than in any other, and in the periodical world which Eliot entered in 1917 it was doubly difficult since literary theory was practically non-existent. The general consistency, therefore, which he has kept upon the premises which he has allowed himself, is a feat which evidences skill, and, if not conformity to well-defined principles, at least adherence to some firmly held pattern of thought.

Perhaps no text verifies this statement better than the one which we shall next consider. When we probe for the answer to the question how affective meanings are translated into poetry, we are confronted with Eliot's well-known description of the *objective correlative*:

> The only way of expressing emotion in the form of art is by finding an "objective correlative"; in other words, a set of objects, a situation, a chain of events which shall be the formula of that *particular* emotion; such that when the external facts, which must terminate in sensory experience, are given, the emotion is immediately evoked. . . . The artistic "inevitability" lies in this complete adequacy of the external to the emotion. . . .[102]

This is a capital text for Eliot and one which requires careful

---

[102] *Sel. Essays,* p. 145. Mario Praz in his study of Dante and Eliot in the *Southern Review,* II (1937), 527-38, refers this text back to Ezra Pound's *The Spirit of Romance,* p. 5: "Poetry is a sort of inspired mathematics, which gives us equations, not for abstract figures, triangles, spheres, and the like, but equations for the human emotions." Pound in turn may have heard T. E. Hulme discuss some such idea, because in *Speculations* there is the following, p. 134: "In prose as in algebra concrete things are embodied in signs or counters which are moved about according to rules, without being visualized at all in the process. . . . Poetry, in one aspect at any rate, may be considered as an effort to avoid this characteristic of prose. It is not a counter language, but a visual concrete one." For other formulations of this principle in Eliot's criticism, see *Sac. Wood,* p. 161; *Sel. Essays,* p. 189; *After Strange Gods,* p. 59. With Eliot's *penchant* for finding words and phrases in out-of-the-way corners, it is not too improbable to suppose that he might have adapted this term, *objective correlative,* from Walt Whitman's 1855 "Preface" to *Leaves of Grass,* American Writers Series (N. Y.: American Book Co., 1934), p. 333: "The prudence of the greatest poet . . . matches every thought or act by its correlative. . . ."

correlation with the rest of his theory if an adequate understanding of his position is to be presented. There are three large points to be considered: first, the kinds of emotion that are expressed in poetry; secondly, the process by which this is accomplished; and thirdly, the end for which it is accomplished. From the foregoing sections of this study it is easy to conclude that Eliot accepts "with the vast majority of his contemporaries the modern dogma that the artist is primarily concerned with emotion."[103] But Eliot has consistently maintained since 1918 that the affective *exprimend,* or the affectivity which is to be expressed, is not the poet's personal emotions. The emotion of art is "depersonalized"; it is emotion significant for poetry. What he calls *significant* emotion "has its life in the poem and not in the history of the poet. The emotion of art is impersonal."[104] Yet, however impersonal the emotion may be, if it is to be significant, it must be *human* emotion. Poetry "must take," Eliot wrote in his essay on Rostand, "genuine and substantial human emotions, such emotions as observation can confirm, typical emotions, and give them artistic form. . . ."[105] The objective poetic emotion then must be a human emotion; that

---

[103] Eliseo Vivas, "The Objective Correlative of T. S. Eliot," *American Bookman,* I (1943), 7.

[104] *Sel. Essays,* p. 22. Cf. also pp. 20-21 of this same essay: "It is not in his personal emotions, the emotions provoked by particular events in his life, that the poet is in any way remarkable or interesting. His particular emotions may be simple, or crude, or flat. The emotion in his poetry will be a very complex thing, but not with the complexity of the emotions of people who have very complex or unusual emotions in life." See also his criticism of the work of M. de Bosschère, "Reflections on Contemporary Poetry," *The Egoist,* IV (1917), 133: "Instead of refining ordinary human emotion (and I do not mean tepid human emotion, but human however intense—in the crude living state) he aims direct at emotions of art." Also his comment upon the dancing of Massine: ". . . the difference between the conventional gesture of the ordinary stage, which is supposed to *express* emotion, and the abstract gesture of Massine, which symbolises emotion, is enormous." "Dramatis Personae," *Criterion,* I (1922-23), 305. Cf. also *Use of Poetry,* p. 155: "Can we say that Shakespeare's poetry is great because of the extraordinary power with which he makes us share them? I enjoy Shakespeare's poetry to the full extent of my capacity for enjoying poetry; but I have not the slightest approach to certainty that I share Shakespeare's feelings; nor am I very much concerned to show whether I do or not."

[105] *Sel. Essays,* p. 41.

is, one which human beings have felt in the past and which they can be made to feel again. This emotion, however, need not be human in the sense that what the poem communicates has been an experience in the poet's personal life. In fact, the poet's personal emotions in so far as they are an expression of his personality are to be sacrificed by combining them with other emotions for the making of the new art emotion. Because Donne seeks for an objective correlative to express *his* [Donne's] personal emotions, Eliot thinks he is a less perfect artist than Andrewes who is so intent upon the object that he is making that the emotion "is wholly evoked by the object of contemplation, to which it is adequate; his emotions wholly contained in and explained by its object." The objective correlative which Andrewes uses perfectly objectifies and adequately symbolizes the emotion he is trying to evoke by it.[106]

In short, the artist must surrender himself "as he is at the moment to something which is more valuable. The progress of an artist is a continual self-sacrifice, a continual extinction of personality."[107] The poet's own emotions are only a starting point; "a good poem, for instance, is not an outburst of pure feeling, but is the result of a more than common power of controlling and manipulating feelings."[108] The strongest writers, like James Joyce, "make their feeling into an articulate external world. . . ."[109] So

---

[106] *Sel. Essays*, p. 341.

[107] *Sel. Essays*, p. 17. Eliot in the essay on "Philip Massinger" makes passing reference to Remy de Gourmont's passage, "La vie est un dépouillement," as though in this doctrine of personality he were simply following the lead of the Frenchman. Porteus, however, points out that "Eliot advanced on Remy de Gourmont's advice." What de Gourmont had said in *Le Problème du Style* was: "Le but de l'activité propre d'un homme est de nettoyer sa personnalité, de la laver de toutes les souillures qu'y déposa l'éducation, de la dégager de toutes les empreintes qu'y laissèrent nos admirations adolescentes." P. 104. This is a description of how to prepare a personality. Eliot assumes that one has a personality and must be ready to sacrifice it for the good of art. For other texts in which he discusses this question, see *Sel. Essays*, p. 157, 217; *Use of Poetry*, p. 154; "Introduction" to *Le Serpent*, tr. by Mark Wardle (London: Cobden-Sanderson, 1924), p. 12. Eliot covered this ground again in "The Poetry of Yeats," *The Southern Review*, VII (1941-42), 446.

[108] "The Idealism of Julien Benda," *The New Republic*, LVIII (1928), 107.

[109] "Ulysses, Myth and Order," *The Dial*, LXXV (1923), 482.

it is not the feelings of the poet but the "pattern which he makes of his feelings, that is the centre of value."[110]

The poem has its origin in the affective life of the poet, the efficient cause of the poem. The usual expressionistic theory is that the *exprimend* is a reality in the psychological life of the poet, the *expressor;* but that the process of expression effects a transition of this *exprimend* into expressive matter, so that somehow an identification of the two takes place. Eliot does not hold fully with this conception. His theory is that the *exprimends* are a complex of affective stimuli, some of which have their origin in the poet, but that the *expressum* has an ontological reality of its own.

The very term, *objective correlative,* points to the fact that poetry contains references to things in the objective world; and Eliot has specified from time to time that this objectivity constitutes a distinguishing note in the formal characteristics of poetry: "a poem, in some sense, has its own life."[111] That is why when Eliot has consciously pointed to a process in relation to poetry it is always one of "making." The artist, he wrote in 1924, "expresses his personality indirectly through concentrating upon a task which is a task in the same sense as the making of an efficient engine or the turning of a jug or a table-leg."[112]

---

[110] *Le Serpent, op. cit.,* p. 12.

[111] *Sac. Wood,* p. x.

[112] *Sel. Essays,* p. 114. In 1920 he wrote in a description of Blake's method of composition: "He has an idea (a feeling, an image), he develops it by accretion or expansion, alters his verse often, and hesitates often over the final choice. The idea, of course, simply comes, but upon arrival it is subjected to prolonged manipulation." *Ibid.,* p. 318. As a craftsman, the poet has no esoteric knowledge. Eliot confesses that he can only pretend to know as much about versifying as any other artisan such as a carpenter or a painter can know about their crafts (*Ezra Pound,* 1928, p. xxiii). Reviewing Maritain's *Situation de la poésie* in *The New English Weekly,* XV (1939), 27, he wrote: "A poet who has no other interest than writing poetry, and only lives, experiences, and uses his mind for the purposes of providing himself with something to write about, is in a very bad case; as is also the poet who is only interested in the 'interior discovery' of himself and not at all in the occupation of *making* something." See also *Kipling* (1943), p. 18: "Most of us are interested in the form for its own sake—not apart from the content, but because we aim at making something which shall first of all be. . . ."

This objective structure, however, is not made as an end in itself; for Eliot it has a functional operation to perform. And "this function is not intellectual but emotional."[113] It serves as a sign or "formula" for the "objective 'poetic emotion.' " For the receptor, an act of perceiving, similar to the one described for the way the poet uses thought, is necessary for the reception of the poem. Cognitional references which are given by the objective correlative are there merely to present external facts which must terminate in affective experience. Thus the artistic emotion is evoked. Eliot's contention is that if the poem is well-made, that is, if the objective correlative is adequate to the emotion presented, there is an artistic "inevitability" or intensity achieved.[114] Both Shakespeare and the writers of the Greek dramas realized this aim completely. "We often feel with Shakespeare," Eliot wrote in *John Dryden,* "and now and then with lesser contemporaries, that the dramatic action on the stage is the symbol and shadow of some more serious action in a world of feeling more real than ours."[115] "Behind the dialogue of Greek drama we are always conscious of a concrete visual actuality, and behind that of a specific emotional actuality."[116] In short, as Eliot declared in "Kipling Redivivus," "the emotion is 'there' simply, coldly independent of the author, of the audience, there and forever like Shakespeare's and Aeschylus' emotions."[117]

The degree of success or failure in correlation between the objects referred to in the poem and the art emotion is in direct ratio to the precision or vagueness of the references.[118] If the object is precise, so will the emotion be; the opposite effect will

---

[113] *Sel. Essays,* p. 138.

[114] Cf. Eliseo Vivas' criticism of this in *The American Bookman, op. cit.,* 11: "But if there is one fact for which we have ample evidence in aesthetics today it is the fact that no artist, however skilful, can possibly control the subjective affective responses of his readers, and this is all the truer to the extent to which the culture to which either poet or reader belongs (or both of course) is complex and in a state of flux, and where therefore to accidental personal idiosyncrasies must be added the differences caused by heterogeneity of social determinants."

[115] *John Dryden* (1932), p. 32.

[116] *Sel. Essays,* p. 68. Cf. de Gourmont, *Le Problème du Style,* p. 164: "Un beau vers porte avec lui son émotion propre, qui est l'émotion esthétique."

[117] "Kipling Redivivus," *The Athenaeum* (May, 1919), 297.

[118] *Sel. Essays,* p. 299.

result if there is "mistiness of the feeling and . . . vagueness of its object." That is why "prose writers may be concerned with ideals, but the poet is always concerned with actuality."[119] In brief, the objective correlative, though composed of cognitive references, and, consequently, stimulating cognitions in the receptor, is important not for these but for the affective meaning which these evoke. Every point arrived at in this study so far has aimed in this direction. But in order to come closer to a realization of what the *differentia* of poetry may be, one must next determine how this affective meaning is produced.

The cohesion of the various objects which make the objective correlative is not a haphazard one, albeit in poetry there is always "a degree of heterogeneity of material" which must be unified.[120] Eliot explained this unification in "The Metaphysical Poets":

> When the poet's mind is perfectly equipped for its work, it is constantly amalgamating disparate experience; the ordinary man's experience is chaotic, irregular, fragmentary. The latter falls in love, or reads Spinoza, and these two experiences have nothing to do with each other, or with the noise of the typewriter or the smell of cooking; in the mind of the poet these experiences are always forming new wholes.[121]

---

[119] *After Strange Gods,* p. 30. Cf. "The Silurist," *The Dial,* LXXXIII (1927), 262: "In short, the emotion of Herbert is clear, definite, mature, and sustained; whereas the emotion of Vaughan is vague, adolescent, fitful, and retrogressive." In *The Chapbook* (1920), 4, Eliot had defined poetry as "an art, that is to say . . . a means of communicating those direct feelings peculiar to art, which range from amusement to ecstasy." Ezra Pound would restrict the pleasure of art to ecstasy alone. "Great art is made, not to please, but to call forth, or create, an ecstasy. The finer the quality of this ecstasy, the finer the art: only secondary art relies on its pleasantness." *The Spirit of Romance,* p. 81. Eliot is much broader in his "range." He chides Dryden for limiting the subject of an heroic poem to "love and valour" (*Sel. Essays,* p. 215). In the review of Lucas' edition of the *Complete Works of Webster* (*The Criterion,* VII, 1928, 158) he speaks of the bitterness and savageness and rage of the major Elizabethan dramatists. In *Sel. Essays,* p. 292 he describes Lucretius as having a savage austerity and Catullus an intense levity. Dryden is the great master of contempt, Pope the great master of hatred, and Swift, the great master of disgust.

[120] *Sel. Essays,* p. 285.

[121] *Ibid.,* p. 287.

All of the poet's experiences whether they are intellectual, affective, or sensory become the raw material for the poet. They conjoin to form a new unity for him.[122] The mechanism which combines these various psychological effects is the poetic sensibility which translates them into affects. This faculty Eliot has defined as "the sensitiveness necessary to record and bring to convergence on a . . . point a multitude of fleeting but universal feelings."[123] When this complex of affective stimuli is completed we have the objective poetic emotion. But the center of attraction for Eliot must be a "point" and this point can only be a complex of cognitive references which is ultimately named by the objective correlative. Because Eliot looks upon this art emotion as composed of elements not necessarily experienced by the poet as an actual life situation, he could write that "emotions which [the poet] has never experienced will serve his turn as well as those familiar to him."[124]

---

[122] From time to time Eliot has designated the following as "matter" for poetry: "emotions and feelings," *Sel. Essays*, p. 18; "thought," *ibid.*, p. 287; "actual life," *ibid.*, p. 111; "a view of life," *ibid.*, p. 155; "oratory," *John Dryden* (1932), p. 17; ". . . the emotions and feelings of the writer himself, which, for that writer are simply material which he must accept," *The Dial*, LXXV, 482; "vision," *Sac. Wood*, p. 170; "personal emotion, personal experience," *Le Serpent*, p. 14; "ideas," *A Garland for John Donne*, p. 11. Sometimes as in the case of Lucretius, the philosophy which he uses is "not rich enough in variety of feeling . . . to supply the material for a wholly successful poem," *Sac. Wood*, p. 162. Eliot maintains that if a poet is honest in accepting the feelings which come to him in various stages of life, there "is no reason why a poet's inspiration or material should fail" before senility. The poet is living in a different world in every decade of his life and thus "the material of his art is continually renewed." *Southern Review*, VII, 448.

[123] *Sel. Essays*, p. 352. Cf. Remy de Gourmont's definition of *sensibilité*, *Le Problème*, p. 107: ". . . et, par sensibilité, j'entends, ici comme partout, le pouvoir général de sentir tel qu'il est inégalement développé en chaque être humain. La sensibilité comprend la raison elle-même, qui n'est que de la sensibilité cristallisée." See also "The Hawthorne Aspect," *The Shock of Recognition*, ed. Edmund Wilson (New York: Doubleday, Doran Co., 1943), p. 862: "Hawthorne and James have a kind of sense, a receptive medium, which is not of sight. Not that they fail to make you see, so far as necessary, but sight is not the essential sense. They perceive by antennae; and the 'deeper psychology' is here."

[124] *Sel. Essays*, p. 21. Cf. "In Memoriam," *Essays, Ancient & Modern*, p. 181: ". . . for a poet with dramatic gifts, a situation quite remote from his personal experience may release the strongest emotion."

This art emotion is "impersonal" in the sense also that "personal emotion, personal experience, is extended and completed in something impersonal—not in the sense of something divorced from personal experience and passion."[125] To achieve this impersonality, the poet must struggle (and this "alone constitutes life for a poet") "to transmute his personal and private agonies into something rich and strange, something universal and impersonal."[126] At times this extension becomes almost exotic, as in Donne, Poe, and Mallarmé, where there is an "expansion of their sensibility beyond the limits of the normal world, a discovery of new objects proper to sustain new emotions."[127]

But though the constituents of the poetic emotion may be impersonal (in the sense explained above), nevertheless, the unification must take place in the poetic sensibility if this emotion is to be adequate for poetry. Eliot reprehends Beaumont and Fletcher because the evocative quality of their verse "depends upon a clever appeal to emotions and associations which they have not themselves grasped; it is hollow."[128] The poet's sensibility gathers the feelings which are attached to the multitude of experiences which all men undergo in like circumstances. Because these feelings are available to all men, Eliot calls them "universal." Because they are feelings, they are necessarily fleeting. This ephemerality is the reason why they can be lost and why it is the duty of the poet to be constantly recovering them. By gathering these feelings together and unifying them, the poet achieves not a personal emotion but a new art emo-

---

[125] *Le Serpent,* p. 14. Cf. "Byron," *From Anne to Victoria,* p. 617: "What puts the last cantos of *Don Juan* at the head of Byron's works is, I think, that the subject matter gave him at last an adequate object for a genuine emotion. The emotion is hatred of hypocrisy; and if it was reinforced by more personal and petty feelings, the feelings of the man who as a boy had known the humiliation of shabby lodgings with an eccentric mother, . . . this mixture at the origin of his attitude towards English society only gives it greater intensity."

[126] *Sel. Essays,* p. 137. Cf. *Use of Poetry,* p. 126: ". . . what we experience as readers is never exactly what the poet experienced, nor would there be any point in its being, though certainly it has some relation to the poet's experience. What the poet experienced is not poetry but poetic material."

[127] "Note sur Mallarmé et Poe," tr. par Ramon Fernandez, *La Nouvelle Revue Française,* XXVI (1926), 525.

[128] *Sel. Essays,* p. 156.

tion to serve as the *exprimend* which clings about a complex of cognitive references and which the objective correlative translates into the words of a poem. As we have shown, when a poem is *musical* (that is, when the sound and meaning have been patterned), there is a communication of the poetic emotion through the perfect union of the musical pattern of the sound and the musical pattern of the secondary meaning of the words, "the musical pattern of emotional overtones." Although Eliot has repudiated the idea that poetry communicates, his rejection of this theory is based upon his refusal to concede that poetry primarily communicates specific cognitions for didactic purposes. This is not the important communication which poetry achieves.

His theory of the communication which is accomplished in poetry is perhaps best explained by a text in *The Use of Poetry* and this text in turn illuminates further his concept of the poetic emotion:

> And what is the experience that the poet is so bursting to communicate? By the time it has settled down into a poem it may be so different from the original experience as to be hardly recognizable. The "experience" in question may be the result of a fusion of feelings so numerous, and ultimately so obscure in their origins, that even if there be communication of them, the poet may hardly be aware of what he is communicating; and what is there to be communicated was not in existence before the poem was completed. "Communication" will not explain poetry. I will not say that there is not always some varying degree of communication in poetry, or that poetry could exist without communication taking place.[129]

The "experience in question" must undoubtedly be an affective one, since Eliot states that it is "the result of a fusion of feelings." If "what is there to be communicated was not in existence before the poem was completed," however, then the objective poetic emotion is not just one emotion which is operative throughout the whole process. Rather the poem must be a series of objective correlatives each one of which refers to a cognitive reference

---

[129] *Use of Poetry,* p. 138.

around which affective *exprimends* converge in the poetic sensibility. That is one of the reasons why throughout this study the term, *affective meanings,* has been used. Eliot does not think that the function of a poem is to communicate an emotion, but rather that a series of affective meanings unite to form a "unity of sentiment." The affective meanings, like the cognitive meanings, are not intended to elicit the "same response from all readers."[130] The poet can only hope to achieve a unity to which receptors will respond according to their capacity.

The function of each objective correlative is to communicate its particular emotion, but each correlative is just one affective sign in the poem as a whole. Since the ultimate achievement of the unity of sentiment depends in some cases upon "various feelings, inhering for the writer in particular words or phrases or images," the unity of sentiment cannot be completed until the poem has been written. For these reasons, Eliot insists that the process of writing poetry is one of making an object rather than a process either of expression or communication. If it were one of expression, then the art emotion would be completely personal in the sense that the poet as efficient cause and the emotion as formal cause would be identical. This Eliot does not concede. For him *exprimends* become impersonal by being extended into the objective world through the objective references in the poem. On the other hand by insisting that the function of poetry is not *primarily* to communicate cognitions but affective responses, Eliot refuses to consider the process as one of cognitive communication since he realizes that this would not ensure uniformity of emotional response.

3. STRUCTURES OF MEANING IN POETRY, PROSE, AND VERSE

Poetry in its intrinsic nature, as we have seen from the preceding section, has an indubitable alliance for Eliot with the affective meanings which the objective correlatives convey. In the whole poem, which may also be a correlative which is structuralized from a succession of these, what is the principle of their organization?

---

[130] *Kipling* (1943), p. 18.

Does the structure of meaning of poetry differ from the structure of meaning of prose? In the *Chapbook* essay, "Prose and Verse," there is a cryptic sentence which reads: "We seem to see clearly enough that prose is allowed to be 'poetic'; we appear to have overlooked the right of poetry to be 'prosaic.' "[131] Prose then may carry affective meanings as well as poetry. Conversely, Eliot suggests that poetry may be as intellectual as prose in its references, but that these references are made not for the sake of communicating their meanings but for the sake of the structure which is the poem. In this same essay we find Eliot adamant against a distinction between prose and poetry based upon language of "emotional and imagination" for poetry and "language of thought and ratiocination" for prose. But in the section entitled "Logic and Imagination," he expanded his notions on the structure of meaning in poetry by noting:

> The work of poetry is often said to be performed by the use of images; by a cumulative succession of images each fusing with the next; or by the rapid and unexpected combination of images apparently unrelated, which have their relationship enforced upon them by the mind of the author. This appears to be true, but it does not follow that there are two distinct faculties, one of imagination and one of reason, one of poetry and one of prose, or that "feeling," in a work of art, is any less an intellectual product than is "thought."[132]

Here Eliot acquiesces in the notion that images "almost always" perform the "work" of poetry, but that does not imply that objective correlative is merely another name for image. Eliot criticizes Shelley, for instance, for not *using* his images; they are only decorative bits: ". . . when Shelley has some definite statement to make, he simply says it; keeps his images on one side and his meanings on the other."[133] There are two ways in which images may be utilized: first, in rapid succession; and next, by unexpected combinations. But the production of the effect of poetry, *feeling,*

---

[131] *The Chapbook,* No. 22 (1921), 5.

[132] *Ibid.,* p. 9.

[133] "A Note on Richard Crashaw," *For Lancelot Andrewes* (N. Y.: Doubleday, Doran & Co., 1929), p. 136.

Eliot holds is not less an intellectual task than the effort expended upon prose. Imagination alone is unable to produce poetry; but when the poet combines reason with imagination, his mind "becomes a fine and delicate tool for an operation on the sensible world."[134]

The *Anabase* is ostensibly an example of the first way in which images may be utilized, and the poetry of Donne illustrates the second. The structure of feeling that results from the poems of Donne is more obvious than in most poets, Eliot intimates in his many critiques of his work, because the poetic sensibility of Donne is more acute. The structure that results in his work is not a structure for the sake of thought but a structure of thought for the sake of feeling. When the thought and the feeling are successfully fused, the feeling is fixed and "concentrates into one intense impression."[135]

Since this is the dominant purpose of poetry, Eliot proposes in the "Preface" to the *Anabase* that one of the best ways to achieve this is to suppress the "links in the chain" of explanatory and connecting matter. Then there will be a "cumulative succession of images each fusing with the next." "Such a sequence of images and ideas" will be fashioned by the "logic of the imagination" rather than a "logic of concepts."[136] But, although Eliot disclaims reduc-

---

[134] "Beyle and Balzac," *The Athenaeum* (May 30, 1919), 392.

[135] *Anabase*, p. [63].

[136] *Ibid.*, p. [63]. Although the idea embodied in the phrase, "logic of the imagination," is not new (cf. Pater's "reasoning imagination"), the phrase is provocative. It is interesting, therefore, to see Valéry's inclusion of it in his "Introduction à la Méthode de Leonard de Vinci," *Les Divers Essais sur Leonard de Vinci* (Paris: La Librairie d'Amateurs, Gibert Jeune, 1931), p. 104: "Je crois également,—peut-être est-ce beaucoup s'avancer!—que le fameuse et séculaire question du plein et du vide peut se rattacher à la conscience ou à l'inconscience de cette *logique imaginative*." Cf. also de Gourmont, *Le Problème du Style*, p. 70. See too W. P. Ker, *Form and Style in Poetry*, *op. cit.*, p. 181: "The apprehension of the arts must be through a kind of intuitive reason, not through the understanding you apply to a chain of evidence. The arts are an attempt of the human mind to get away from finitude, from 'creeping on from point to point,' to use Tennyson's expression. Artistic reasoning is the antithesis to the ordinary syllogism proceeding from one proposition to another; in the arts the mind is exalted and finds a new power, seeing things at a glance and easily, instead of having to take time to work them out."

ing the elements of poetry to images, he calls the principle of structure "logic of imagination." This phrase may be just a manner of speaking; a phrase used in the effort to distinguish poetical unity from the logical cohesion found in other kinds of discourse. But it suggests that what makes poetry something more than a succession of images is some cognitive and quasi-intellectual principle. By using the word *logic,* Eliot implies that the structure must be consistent in order to achieve unity, and this work must always be performed by the intellect. Again, Eliot decries attributing poetry to the imagination and prose to the intellect; and, further, he asserted "that 'feeling'," in a work of art, is no less "an intellectual product than is 'thought.'"

To produce the affective meaning of poetry most forcefully, Eliot holds that there may be poetry written in which the images are so compact and so fused together that the discourse which would ordinarily link them is dropped out. Some modern poetry is like this and if the effect which the poetry is trying to produce is not understood the reader may be bewildered. He will puzzle "his head for a kind of 'meaning' which is not there, and is not meant to be there."[137] The task of the poet in writing such poetry is to order "the arrangement of images."[138] But in most poetry, the discourse is not simply a succession of images. Eliot himself has pleaded that we should not overlook the right of poetry to be prosaic. In other words, granting that a succession of images appeals to the imagination alone, not all poetry is written in this fashion. If a discourse, therefore, is written in verse sound structure, but the meaning structure is primarily cognitive in quality, will this discourse be called *poetry* or *verse?*

Since it has been shown that poetry is quite obviously linked with affective meanings, the word *verse,* as it occurs in Eliot's criticism, becomes an object to scrutinize. Does he consider verse not as associated exclusively with sound structure but as containing some meaning, and therefore, capable of being a generic form of discourse? Certainly, when we turn to his latest work on Kip-

---

[137] *Use of Poetry,* p. 150.
[138] *Anabase,* p. [63].

ling,[139] we find that the word *verse* has put on new dignity and has broadened in its connotations. Toward the end of the essay is a lengthy passage which explains Eliot's position:

> I make no apology for having used the terms "verse" and "poetry" in a loose way: so that while I speak of Kipling's work as verse and not as poetry, I am still able to speak of individual compositions as poems, and also to maintain that there is "poetry" in the "verse." Where terminology is loose, where we have not the vocabulary for distinctions which we feel, our only precision is found in being aware of the imperfection of our tools, and of the different senses in which we are using the same words. It should be clear that when I contrast "verse" with "poetry" I am not, in this *context,* implying a value judgment. I do not mean, here, by verse, the work of a man who would write poetry if he could: I mean by it something which does what "poetry" could not do. . . . And I make the claim, that in speaking of Kipling we are entitled to say *"great* verse."[140]

Now if we use the terms which are at our disposal, *poetry,*

---

[139] A systematic study of Eliot's prose reveals that most of his enthusiasms are of long standing. When he writes an essay on a particular author or aspect of technique, it has usually been preceded by alarums and excursions which are either casual notes or incidental remarks inserted during the discussion of other topics. Such is the thread of interest which Eliot has shown in Kipling. In 1919 he noted that Kipling's poetry was "the poetry of oratory; it is music just as the words of the orator or preacher are music; they persuade, not by reason but by emphatic sound" ("Kipling Redivivus," *The Athenaeum,* May 9, 1919, pp. 297-298). "Mr. Kipling's Benefit," *The New Criterion,* IV, p. 628 assured us that "the work of Kipling as a whole has a *sense,* a meaning, which few of its readers will trouble to apprehend; but without apprehending which no one is competent to judge its greatness or abate its value." When Kipling's remains were transferred to the Abbey in 1936, Eliot devoted one of the Commentaries in the fifteenth volume of *The Criterion* to him in which he introduced three of the notes which he was to develop later: that Kipling was probably "the greatest writer of short stories in the language," that his handling of verse was so masterful that in some instances he made original contributions; and that "he was a great balladist." (P. 462) Therefore, when we find Eliot editing a portion of Kipling's work in 1943, it is not surprising.

[140] *Ibid.,* p. 35.

prose, and *verse,* and combine these so that the term denoting meaning structure is always first, we may arrive at the following groupings: (A) poetry-verse; (B) prose-verse; (C) poetry-prose; and (D) prose-prose. As we have seen in the "Preface" to the *Anabase,* Eliot contends that poetry may occur in prose sound structure; but even there, he adds that poetry has its own "declamation"; and therefore that it is more normal that poetry should occur in verse (A). Conversely, though verse may exemplify prose-meaning virtues, yet verse seems more naturally consonant with poetic virtues. Likewise, most of the poetry which he quotes and uses to illustrate his points is in verse. Consequently, the natural affinity of poetry for verse and of prose for prose sound structure, makes it also natural that B seems more like poetry than like prose at its normal form, D.

But, in the meaning structure of poetry-prose is there a continuum in the line as there is in that of the sound structure, prose-verse? If so, all speech is not simply either prose or poetry. It would then be possible to have an intermediate range of speech between these two which is neither simply prose nor poetry. Only B and C could occupy this middle range. But if C is really poetry in prose sound structure, it is as much poetry as is A. Therefore, this leaves B as sole possible or normal occupant of the intermediate range. C, Eliot implies, is possible but not normally suitable for this middle range. Therefore, Kipling's verse occupies some part of this intermediate region, B.

Eliot does not question Kipling's technical ability; he is acknowledged a master craftsman. "Kipling could handle, from the beginning to the end, a considerable variety of metres and stanza forms with perfect competence; he introduces remarkable variations of his own. . . ."[141] What Kipling did, and here we have another approach to a classification of his work, was to use verse as an instrument—"the poem is something which is intended to *act*—and for the most part his poems are intended to elicit the same response from all readers, and only the response which they can make in common."[142] Because Kipling's work carries a com-

---

[141] *Ibid.,* p. 34.
[142] *Ibid.,* p. 18.

municative power which is intended to persuade, Eliot denies it
the title of poetry. His great distinction here is based upon final
cause or purpose. Writers, he comments, "who are interested in
the form for its own sake—not apart from the content, but because [they] aim at making something which shall first of all
be,"[143] are interested not in arousing one set response, but in concentrating upon the work itself. "The poet does not aim to excite
. . . but to set something down; the state of the reader is merely
that reader's particular mode of perceiving what the poet has
caught in words."[144] This only corroborates what Eliot has consistently maintained: that poetry is not for communication. Whatever is communicated will affect readers according to their capacity
for response—not because the author has desired to call forth a
uniform reaction. Its effects vary according to the individual
variations of the receptors and it is no part of the poet's task in
writing poetry to take these into account.[145] The verse of Kipling
terminates in a final cause which is extrinsic to it. "The end of
the enjoyment of poetry" for Eliot "is a pure contemplation from
which all the accidents of personal emotion are removed."[146] Kipling, in other words, appeals to the reader's own emotions. For
Eliot the receptor in contemplating poetry should not be moved
by his own emotions but by the "emotions of art." This is "to see
the object as it really is."[147] Because Kipling's work is "intended
to *act*," and because it is deemed capable of performing this action,
one can only conclude that *verse* in this context connotes a dis-

---

[143] *Ibid.*, p. 17.

[144] *Sac. Wood*, p. 170. Cf. also *Sel. Essays*, p. 24: "I do not deny that art
may be affirmed to serve ends beyond itself; but art is not required to be
aware of these ends, and indeed performs its function, whatever that may
be, according to various theories of value, much better by indifference to
them."

[145] Many people think from the obscurity in his own work that Eliot is
completely indifferent to his reading public. To think this is to ignore his
half-wistful remark (which is typical of others) in *The Use of Poetry*, p. 31:
"It is one thing to write in a style which is already popular, and another to
hope that one's writing may eventually become popular."

[146] *Sac. Wood*, pp. 14-15.

[147] *Ibid.*, p. 15. See also, *Ibid.*, p. 12: "But a literary critic should have no
emotions except those immediately provoked by a work of art. . . ."

course which has prose structure of meaning but whose sound structure possesses a strong affinity for poetry. Kipling's verse is *not* poetry because he used it for a "public purpose" and because of the "subordination of musical interest."

If we accept this use of Eliot's term, then we may challenge his right to demand a fourth term in the essay on the *Anabase*. There he stated that prose and poetry were forms of discourse which might take either metrical or non-metrical sound structures. Recognizing the awkwardness of this terminology, he called for a fourth term which would indicate *prose* as a mode as well as a form, implying always, that verse referred only to the level of sound. When verse assumes a meaning structure, and it is used now in one context and now in another, just as much awkwardness and ambiguity occur as one experiences with the word *prose*. From the essay on Kipling we may assume not two but three generic forms of discourse: *prose, poetry,* and *verse*. Eliot admits that terminology is loose; but though it may help Eliot to explain his ideas of Kipling, is using such a supercharged word as *verse* in this way ever going to clarify matters?

With the appearance of this new connotation for *verse* the problem of the *differentia* of poetry assumes a new aspect. If it is to be a real *differentia,* it must distinguish poetry not only from prose but from verse as well. The next chapter will be devoted to this and to the remaining problem: the tradition into which Eliot's criticism falls.

CHAPTER IV

THE CLARIFICATION OF THE CENTER:

THE *Differentia* OF POETRY

> The task of criticism will be . . . not only to expand
> its borders but to clarify its centre. . . .
>
> T. S. Eliot

I

Emphasis upon the affective meaning of poetry would seem then to be for Eliot the mark differentiating it from prose. But since meaning must imply cognitional meaning as well as affective meaning and Eliot has said that this cognitional meaning cannot be eliminated entirely from poetry nor affective meaning from prose, a question arises as to when this affective meaning is so apparent that the discourse, even though written in prose sound structure, is unmistakably poetry. Furthermore, since the term *verse* may denote a generic form of discourse, it is necessary to find some *differentia* which will set *poetry* apart from this *verse* as well as from *prose*. In the section on structure of meaning, a method of "poetic" structure was suggested: an elimination of the " 'links in the chain' of explanatory and connecting matter." Justification for this method was based upon the effect achieved; it "coincides and concentrates into one intense impression."[1] Now, if we turn to the essay on Kipling, the distinction that Eliot makes between Kipling's work which is verse[2] and that which is poetry is just

---

[1] *Anabase,* p. [63].

[2] To list adequately all the references in which Eliot uses *verse* as connoting a structure of meaning would require the mechanism of a concordance rather than that of a footnote. As samples of this use, consider: The title of the *Chapbook* essay, "Prose and Verse"; *Sel. Essays,* p. 179: "As in the passage from *A Woman Killed with Kindness* quoted above, the verse, which nowhere bursts into a flame of poetry, is yet economical and tidy, and formed to extract all the dramatic value possible from the situation." "Johnson's 'London,' " p. 304: We may even say that the originality of some poets has

this note of *intensity*. "There is no need," he wrote, "to show that Kipling's verse reaches from time to time the intensity of 'poetry.' " If intensity marks the difference between *poetry* and *verse,* it also, as we have hinted in Chapter III, differentiates *poetry* from *prose.* Andrewes' sermons, which according to Eliot contain poetry, are marked by relevant intensity. When intensity appears in prose, however, it is apt to be so diffused throughout the whole work that its appearance is scarcely discernible. In Gibbon's *History* for instance "it takes seven volumes for communication."[3] What then characterizes the intensity of poetry?

In the essay on Kipling, Eliot ascribed to poetry a "musical pattern of emotional overtones." As we have seen, the patterns necessary for poetry are rhythmic and affective *expriments.* How are these to be reconciled with the *prosaic* which is found in the meaning structure of verse and which in some poetry is highly commended by Eliot? Likewise, what relation does intensity bear to these elements? A passage in *The Music of Poetry* harmonizes these apparently incompatible characteristics and clarifies Eliot's concept of poetry considerably:

> . . . in a poem of any length, there must be transitions between passages of greater and less intensity, to give a rhythm of fluctuating emotion essential to the musical structure of the whole; and the passages of less intensity will be, in relation to the level on which the total poem operates, prosaic—so that, in the sense implied by that context, it may be said that no poet can write a poem of amplitude unless he is a master of the prosaic.[4]

Every discourse, Eliot holds, contains the same elements but in varying proportions. When the sound structure of a discourse veers sharply from regularity in its rhythms and the cognitive quality of

---

consisted in their finding a way of saying in verse what no one else had been able to say except in prose written or spoken." "The Poetic Drama," *The Athenaeum* (May 14, 1921), 635: "He must stand quite alone: which means that he must, if he can, write poetry (not merely good blank verse) *at every moment.*"

[3] *The Chapbook,* No. 22 (1921), 4.
[4] *Music of Poetry,* p. 18.

the meaning structure is intended to convey knowledge of some sort while the affective meaning is negligible, that discourse is prose. If the sound structure follows a rhythmic pattern, or, at least, approaches regularity and the meaning structure like prose contains a message which is intended to *act,* that discourse is verse. But if in a sound structure which is perfectly adapted to it the affective meaning is "fixed with intensity" in a cognitive meaning structure, that discourse is poetry. The greater intensity of poetry is apparent when the affective meaning is more clearly marked than the cognitive, though the latter is always present in some degree, and these in turn are reinforced by the sound structure. In the light of this explanation such a statement as that in the "Preface" to the *Anabase* becomes clearer: that "poetry may occur . . . at any point along a line of which the formal limits are 'verse' and 'prose.' " Now we can see that the line represents discourse which may be written in prose or verse sound structure and prose or verse meaning structure, but which becomes poetry at such moments as there is this greater intensity. Therefore, the provocative use of "occurs" is exactly right.

So, once more, Eliot enunciates a principle of relativity. Since intensity is present in every discourse, it is only when intensity is greater that poetry occurs. As the intensity diminishes, the discourse moves toward the prosaic. Even in the verse of Dryden and Pope "there is movement between greater and less intensity."[5] As the intensity must oscillate more widely in a long poem than in a short one, to write a long poem involves a mastery of prose. Eliot does not think with Poe that the long poem should not be written. No one, he says, objects to the length of the *Divine Comedy,* the *Odyssey,* or the *Aeneid.* "The poems I have just mentioned have, in different degrees, the movement toward and from intensity which is life itself."[6] It is this intensity which gives unity to these works—a unity which Milton and Wordsworth lack.[7]

---

[5] *The Chapbook,* No. 22 (1921), pp. 4-5. See also *Use of Poetry,* p. 92: "One does not expect a poem to be equally sustained throughout; and in some of the most successful long poems there is a relation of the more tense to the more relaxed passages, which is itself part of the pattern of beauty."

[6] *The Chapbook,* No. 22, 5.

[7] Dryden too believes in this fluctuation of intensity. Cf. the "Preface" to *Troilus and Cressida, Essays,* ed. W. P. Ker, I, p. 221.

Though Eliot considers the affective meaning a necessary element for poetry, as this study has repeatedly shown, and though one might be led to think that he thus links intensity exclusively with affectivity, investigation proves that he does not associate intensity solely with emotion, but in various texts he has commented upon the results which are produced when intensity is linked with each of the elements of poetry.

In relation to imagery intensity makes it "represent something much more than itself." Thus Baudelaire not merely used imagery of common life but he elevated it to the first intensity.[8] He, like Shakespeare and Dante, became "the voice of his time" not because he used the "satanism" of the Black Mass which was very much in the air but because in him it meant "something else." While using the same paraphernalia as other poets of his day, his intensity expands its symbolism beyond the limit of "all that of which he is conscious."

In the review of *Nightwood* there is a linking of sound structure and intensity. There we are told that Miss Barnes's "prose rhythm may be more or less complex or elaborate" according to her purposes; but "whether simple or complex, it is what raises the matter to be communicated, to the first intensity."[9]

That the intensity of poetry is likewise connected in some way with the poet's psychological responses Eliot intimates in the notes on the odes of Cowley. Cowley's world was such that "no object of belief" was "capable of eliciting from him a response of the highest poetic intensity." Because Cowley responded to Hobbes' attack on tradition, Eliot thinks there is more "adequacy" in the ode to Hobbes than there is in "The Mistress."[10]

But Eliot does not necessarily think that the emotion of the poet is responsible for the adequacy of the ode. As a substantiation of this statement one may recall that in 1917 Eliot observed that "the distinction between poetry and prose must be a technical distinction; and future refinements of both poetry and prose can

---

[8] *Intimate Journals,* tr. Christopher Isherwood, "Introduction" by T. S. Eliot (N. Y.: Random House, 1930), p. 16.

[9] *The Criterion,* XVI (1936), 561.

[10] "Notes on Two Odes of Cowley," *Studies in Honor of Sir H. J. C. Grierson, op. cit.,* p. 238.

only draw the distinction more clearly."[11] In glossing what Eliot means by "technique" or "technical" we find that to designate a work *poetry* is not a question of metrical structure nor of the cognitive references utilized but rather one of the way "in which this subject-matter is treated."

Perhaps, he suggested in the *Chapbook* essay, two qualities or sets of qualities might be found and "the best literature, verse and prose," could be divided "into two parts which shall exemplify these two qualities."[12] Each group of literary works would then comprehend both verse and prose. Classification would be decided on the basis of whatever qualities are agreed upon as constituting the *differentiae* for the groups. This division would then be effected on the basis of some relation between "technique" and meaning.[13] Seven years later when evaluating the contribution of Ezra Pound, Eliot remarked that he did not "limit the 'art of verse' by the necessary but dangerous word technique."[14] And in that same year, he evaded a definition of *technique* in the following manner:

> . . . in criticizing poetry, we are right if we begin, with what sensibility and what knowledge of other poetry we possess, with poetry as excellent words in excellent arrangement and excellent metre. That is what is called the technique of verse. But we observe that we cannot define even the technique of verse; we cannot say at what point "technique" begins or where it ends; and if we add to it a "technique of feeling," that glib phrase will carry us but little farther.[15]

Since we can know nothing of a "technique of feeling," and since the affective meaning is yet so important for poetry, obviously an impasse would be reached if Eliot referred *intensity* exclusively

---

[11] *The New Statesman,* IX (May 19, 1917), 159.
[12] *The Chapbook,* No. 22, 4.
[13] Cf. "Johnson's 'London,'" *op. cit.,* p. 304. Also *Ezra Pound* (1928), p. xix: ". . . what 'poetry lovers' do not recognize is that their limitation of poetry to the 'poetical' is a modern restriction of the romantic age: the romantic age has decided that a great deal of prose is poetry . . . and conversely that a good deal of poetry is prose."
[14] Isolated Superiority," *The Dial,* LXXXIV (1928), 5
[15] *Sac. Wood,* p. ix. Cf. "Professional, or . . ." *The Egoist,* V (1918), 61.

to the poet's personal emotions. In "Tradition and the Individual Talent," however, he divorces intensity from pure affectivity in these terms: ". . . it is not the 'greatness,' the intensity, of the emotions, the components, but the intensity of the artistic process, the pressure, so to speak, under which the fusion takes place, that counts."[16] The *differentia* of poetry then becomes a quality which is achieved and recognized by the excellent unity of the work's component elements. As such, it is caught in the work and resides there objectively as a factor for examination by all who are able to discern it.

Does this explanation tally with Eliot's concept of artistic process? As we have seen, in his description of the objective correlative, he united three processes into an amalgam. He cannot be referring to the first of these, the expression of emotion, because he has stated that it is not the intensity of the components to which he is pointing; and this fusion of emotional components takes place not in the poetic object but in the poetic sensibility of the poet. Obviously, no "artistic process" is possible here. Furthermore, he has noted in *The Use of Poetry* that he preferred "not to define, or to test, poetry by means of speculations about its origins; you cannot find a sure test for poetry, a test by which you may distinguish between poetry and mere good verse, by reference to its putative antecedents in the mind of the poet."[17]

Of the second process which he mentions, the communication of the artistic emotion, he has averred that " 'communication' will not explain poetry."[18] Since Eliot does not concede that poetry should impart specific intellectual knowledge nor arouse a uniform reaction, quite clearly no *differentia* could be possible in an area where such deviations are to be expected.

It is in examining "intensity of the artistic object" in conjunction with the process of making an object that the most promising implications for an understanding of Eliot's theory can be discerned. Emotion is necessary for poetry—"the poet must start from his own emotions"—but emotion alone is not enough. There

---

[16] *Sel. Essays*, p. 19. Cf. *supra*, pp. 40, 59, and 95.

[17] *Use of Poetry*, p. 140.

[18] *Ibid.*, p. 138.

must be a structure of thought for the sake of the emotion. Cognitional references are presented by the objective correlative, or as Eliot expressed it in *The Bookman,* "poetry is the creation of a sensuous embodiment." In the process of fusing this structure of thought with emotion, the emotion itself remains no longer a "personal" emotion but becomes an objective "art emotion." The emotion of poetry can, therefore, no longer be identified with the poet's affective reactions. Neither can it be attributed to the response which the work awakens in the reader. It is something which has achieved an objective status by being embodied in a poetic discourse.

Throughout this study the phrase *affective meaning* has been used to describe this art emotion in order to indicate the objectivity which Eliot wishes to attribute to poetry. If objectivity is to be secured, however, something more than mere affectivity is required; a meaning structure which can be impartially contemplated is necessary. Whenever the required elements are successfully fused, Eliot thinks that intensity marks the discourse as poetry; but the presence of this quality is indicative not solely of intense emotions but of intense operations which are largely (though not wholly) "intellectual." The artistic process then which Eliot conceives is perhaps best described as objectifying intensity; and the *differentia* which he acknowledges is the presence in a discourse of this intensity so objectified.

Perhaps this criterion is spontaneously recognized by a "sufficient number of the best minds," who decide what is or what is not poetry. Perhaps it is "tradition" which determines when the artistic process is sufficiently intense. At any rate, by severing the art emotion from the personality of the poet and by attempting to intellectualize in part the artistic process, Eliot has endeavored to establish an objective *differentia* which marks the ontological status of poetry.

II

Before concluding this study one more problem remains to be answered: in what tradition may we place Eliot's theory? He has characterized the two traditions which have directed criticism, at least until the end of the eighteenth century, as the Aristotelian and the Horatian, although he observed in *The Sacred Wood,* "it is far less Aristotle than Horace who has been the model for criticism up to the nineteenth century."[19]

As a protest against the degeneration of modern criticism (that is, roughly speaking, criticism since the beginning of the nineteenth century), Eliot published "The Perfect Critic," in which as one can see from the quotations given in the introduction to this study, his praise of Aristotle is profuse. Eliot's evident desire for reform in criticism and his confessed preference for Aristotle would lead one to ask how far his theory is in accord with the Aristotelian tradition. Throughout his work Eliot has constantly been referring to the discourse of poetry as dynamic.[20] "The poem comes before the form," he wrote in *The Music of Poetry,* "in the sense that a form grows out of the attempt of somebody to say something."[21] As we have seen, Donne and Dryden are lauded because of the use of contemporary speech in their poetry. Donne "introduced into lyric verse a style of conversation, of direct natural speech."[22] "The poetry of a people," Eliot wrote in 1933, "takes its life from the people's speech and in turn gives life to it"; but it is never just speech in the abstract, it is speech which has been formed for a purpose in a structure.[23] How closely the

---

[19] *Sac. Wood,* p. 11.

[20] In 1910 Pound wrote in *The Spirit of Romance,* p. 234: "The spirit of the arts is dynamic. The arts are not passive, nor static, nor, in a sense, are they reflective, though reflection may assist at their birth."

[21] *Mus. of Poetry,* p. 26.

[22] *John Dryden* (1932), p. 12.

[23] Cf. the following: "At one stage the stanza is a right and natural formalization of speech into pattern." *Mus. of Poetry,* p. 25. " 'The language of the middle and lower classes of society' is of course perfectly proper when you are representing *dramatically* the speech of these classes, and then no other language is proper: similarly when you are representing dramatically the language of the upper classes; but on other occasions, it is not the business of the poet to talk like *any* class of society, but like himself— rather better, we hope, than any actual class; though when any class of society happens to have the best word, phrase or expletive for anything, then the poet is entitled to it." *The Use of Poetry,* pp. 71-72. "Those who first found their speech during that war . . . form a second age group. . . ."

speech of poetry must conform to the speech of the poet is determined by various factors: in dramatic poetry, for instance, the "dependence of verse upon speech is much more direct . . . than in any other."[24] The reason for this is that

> in most kinds of poetry, the necessity for its reminding us of contemporary speech is reduced by the latitude allowed for personal idiosyncrasy: a poem by Gerard Hopkins, for instance, may sound pretty remote from the way in which you and I express ourselves—or rather, from the way in which our fathers and grandfathers expressed themselves: but Hopkins does give the impression that his poetry has the necessary fidelity to *his* way of thinking and talking to himself.[25]

From this text we may conclude that to Eliot poetry is a discourse which suggests a voice speaking; there is dynamic reference, though deviation from the normal speech will be determined by the idiosyncrasies of the individual poet. But, as this study has tried to show, since there is such ambiguity apparent in the various structures which we have examined, the first point of enquiry must be: how does Eliot regard this speech? He pointed out in 1928 that "we can only say that a poem in some sense has its own life." In this respect, he would seem to classify poetry as "detached" speech;[26] that is, speech separated by its structure from any actual speech-situation. If we can determine that it is the latter, then we may enquire if he thinks poetry is "imitation" in the same sense as Aristotle—not as one commentator has called it, an "esthetic norm,"[27]—but as an ontological class.

A survey of the forms of poetry in which Eliot has been interested will reveal that the majority of his critical works turn upon

---

The Little Book of Modern Verse (London: Faber & Faber, 1941), p. 6. "Just as, from the beginning, he made and thought his poetry in terms of speech. . . ." *The Southern Review,* VII, 452.

[24] *Mus. of Poetry,* p. 20.

[25] *Ibid.,* p. 20.

[26] For an explanation of this term, see Shipley, *Dictionary,* art. "Voice and Address," p. 617.

[27] F. O. Nolte, " 'Imitation' as an Aesthetic Norm," *Art and Reality* (Lancaster, Pa.: Lancaster Press, Inc., 1942).

two kinds: the drama and the lyric. As to the former he wrote in *The Athenaeum* when reviewing John M. Murry's *Cinnamon and Angelica*: "The poet who now applies himself to the drama. . . will be one with a strong and . . . philosophic conviction in favour of this form. He will be a very conscious poet, with an historical imagination. . . ."[28] The motivation behind this interest in dramatic form "is the consciousness, the construction of the possible meaning, the possible value in feeling which a triumphant poetic drama might have for the sensibilities of the most sensitive contemporary." What he has hinted here, Eliot developed more amply in the conclusion to *The Use of Poetry*: "In a play of Shakespeare you get several levels of significance. For the simplest auditors there is the plot, for the more literary the words and phrasing, for the more musically sensitive the rhythm, and for auditors of greater sensitiveness and understanding a meaning which reveals itself gradually."[29] From the discussion of Eliot's theory in general, we can only surmise that the "meaning which will reveal itself gradually," is a "possible value in feeling." The philosophical conviction in favor of the dramatic form (which he was to call later "the ideal medium for poetry") was, as he pointed out in the Murry review, the realization that in this form the poet could be more objective; or, as he expressed it in 1933, it gives the poet the opportunity "to think his own thoughts behind a tragic or a comic mask."[30] Eliot has utilized this form in two of his finished works, as well as contributing the choruses of *The Rock* and the unfinished fragments of *Sweeney Agonistes*. His own technique, he has admitted, has been derived from Elizabethan and Jacobean dramatists, and his constant concern has been the lack of poetic drama in our day. Furthermore, a general criticism which he has levelled against "contemporary verse" is that most of it "shows a deficiency in lack of any dramatic intent, which might help to correct its imperfectly conceived philosophies and its imperfectly objectified emotions."[31]

---

[28] *The Athenaeum* (May 14, 1920), 635.
[29] *Use of Poetry*, p. 153.
[30] *Ibid.*, p. 154.
[31] *The Criterion*, XI (1931-32), 680.

All of these pointers toward drama would seem to make Eliot particularly susceptible to an Aristotelian theory of poetry, but there is one difficulty which presents itself. Much of Eliot's poetry is lyric. The fragment of the *Poetics,* as we now have it, discusses only dramatic and narrative poetry. Lyric poetry is not mentioned. Bywater in his notes to his 1909 edition links the lyric very definitely with the Greek theory of music:

> Lyric poetry, apart from an occasional reference to the Dithyramb and Nome, or the chorica in tragedy, is ignored in the existing *Poetics;* and there is little or no reason to suppose it to have been discussed in the lost portion of the book. The probability is that, from the importance of its musical element, it belonged in Aristotle's classification of the arts to the theory of *musike* rather than to that of poetry proper.[32]

Another barrier which presents itself is that of the identification by Aristotle of *poesis-mimesis* with *mythos,* or story, within those poetic structures which are discussed in the *Poetics.* How Aristotle would have treated the lyric we do not know. But there are implications for a mimetic theory in the treatment of "manner in which each kind of object is presented"; and, as we hope to show, these same implications are in part to be found in Eliot's theory.

Enumerating the ways in which poetry may be presented, Aristotle says:

> Given both the same means and the same kind of object for imitation, one may either (1) speak at one moment in narrative and at another in an assumed character, as Homer does; or (2) one may remain the same throughout, without any such changes; or (3) the imitators may represent the whole story dramatically, as though they were actually doing the things described.[33] (1448a19-23)

[32] Ingram Bywater, *Aristotle's Poetics* (London: Oxford University Press, 1909), p. 97. From his constant reference to this subject close reading of Bywater's notes would suggest that he is troubled with this explanation and would like to establish lyric as a species of mimetic poetry.

[33] Bywater's translation. For the development of this text I am deeply indebted to Professor La Drière's essay, "Voice and Address," Shipley's *Dictionary,* pp. 615-617.

What must be noted first is the use of the word *imitation* for two purposes: that is, for the re-presenting of the object in speech structure, or the relation to reality of the fictions in the poetry; and secondly, for the application of imitation to voice or voices speaking within that structure. The structure itself may imitate two kinds of object: either action or thought. As Aristotle defined Thought, it is "the power of saying whatever can be said, or what is appropriate to the occasion" (1450b5), and this is, of course, closely connected with what he had to say on Diction: "The Thought of the personages is shown in everything to be effected by their language—in every effort to prove or disprove to arouse emotion (pity, fear, anger, and the like) or to maximize or minimize things'" (1456a36-1456b1). When a Thought is expressed by the characters in a drama, their actions must be compatible with the impression they desire to make, and sometimes in drama actions alone must carry the Thought. In the essay on John Dryden, Eliot has called this the "theatrically dramatic" which exists when "the speech has its equivalent in, or can be projected by, the action and gesture and expression of the actor."[34] With the spoken word, however, the Thought "has to be produced by the speaker and result from his language" (1456b8). And this Eliot has called the "poetic dramatic" and says that it is a value which is "something dramatic in essence which can only be expressed by the word and by the reception of the word."[35] The presentation of the subject-matter by thought as described by Aristotle is the condition of the lyric, and the effects of this form also must be achieved by language alone.

Turning now to a consideration of voice, we see that a structural imitation may be presented first (as Aristotle lists them) by a mixed mode "in which the basic voice is the speaker's own, but other personalities are at times assumed and their voices introduced" in direct quotation.[36] This is called mixed because when the speaker speaks in his own name, using his own voice, it is nonmimetic; when he assumes the voice or voices of other personalities,

---

[34] *John Dryden* (1932,) p. 29.
[35] *Ibid.*, p. 29.
[36] La Drière, Shipley's *Dictionary,* p. 616.

the speech becomes mimetic. This is the mode of most narrative. Next, the mode of pure exposition or pure narration; in this the voice is that of the speaker himself and his is the only voice that is heard. This mode is non-mimetic. The third was the mode designated by the ancients as *mimesis*. "It produces dialogue (as . . . in drama) or, if there be only one assumed voice, 'dramatic' monologue." Since, in most lyric poetry only one voice is heard, if that species is to be assimilated into a mimetic scheme, that voice must be considered not as the voice of the poet himself but as that "of a personality assumed by the speaker in imagination" either as a voice in the mixed or first mode, or as a single speech in the drama of the third mode from which the rest of the structure has been cut off.[37]

---

[37] Among the Greeks since lyric poetry was always associated with music (witness the odes of Pindar and the lyrics of Sappho) and since music was considered a mimetic art, this form raised no problems. When, during the Alexandrian age, lyric forms were becoming dissociated from music, poetry had become assimilated into the rhetorical tradition and remained there throughout the Middle Ages. It was only with the Renaissance and the recovery of the *Poetics* that this type became a problem. Several of the Italian Renaissance critics attempted to explain the lyric as a mimetic form. Among these were Agnolo Segni, who delivered six lectures before the Florentine Academy in 1573, defending the poetry of Petrarch as "true poetic imitation." Because Aristotle did not discuss the lyric, most Renaissance critics equated imitation with drama and narrative exclusively. But Segni argued that poetry does not directly imitate either the universal truths of philosophy or the particular truths of history. He held that "the function of the poet is to give a fictitious reality to the union of unrelated materials; poetry . . . imitates the poet's mental image which conjoins the generic and particular to form an original imaginative construct." Therefore, Segni thought of the fable or *mythos* of Aristotle in the broad sense of "imaginative representation, which may be with or without action." To Segni the voice speaking in the poetry was merely a technical feature for differentiating the various kinds of imitations. For further description of Segni's contribution, see "Agnolo Segni and a Renaissance Definition of Poetry," G. Giovannini, *MLQ*, VI (June, 1945): 167-173. Batteux in the early eighteenth century also offered a description of the lyric as imitation but with characteristic eighteenth century emphasis: ". . . dans la Poésie épique et dramtique on imite les actions & les moeurs; dans le Lyrique, on chante les sentiments, ou les passions imitées. S'il y a ru réel, il se mêle avec ce qui est feint, pour faire un Tout de même nature: la fiction embellit

Whether or not Eliot had any such scheme in mind about the lyric (and from evidence, as we shall see, he probably did not), nevertheless, this fact remains: that in 1920 he wrote: "The natural evolution, for us, would be to proceed in the direction indicated by Browning; to distil the dramatic essences, if we can, and infuse them into some other liquor."[38] Therefore, when Eliot wrote in 1922, ". . . what great poetry is not dramatic? Even the minor writers of the Greek Anthology, even Martial, are dramatic,"[39] what did he mean by dramatic? Was he thinking of mimetic structure in voice and meaning? Certainly, from the great effort he has made to separate poetry from other intellectual disciplines, one might infer that he does not consider poetry as speech of direct exposition. Recalling what he said about Hopkins' poetry will verify this. What his poetry does is to give

---

la verité, & la verité donne du crédit à la fiction." M. Batteux, *Principes de la Litterature* (Paris: Deŝaint & Saillant, 1775), pp. 267-268. Julius Petersen (*Die Wissenschaft von der Dichtung*, Berlin: Junker und Dünnhaupt Verlag, 1939), p. 122 in his systematic approach to theory does not mention Aristotle although he links drama and lyric "in der Darstellung." The point of differentiation in his separation of the species of poetry is divided between voice and meaning: "Jede Eigenschaft für sich allein, oder, wie man ebensogut sagen kann, diese typischen Eigenschaften rechtfertigen eine empirische Trennung der Dichtungsgattungen. Für die Lyrik ist es der Zustand, für die Epik der Bericht, für das Drama der Dialog."

[38] This idea he repeated in the lectures on modern literature which he delivered at Harvard in 1933. Professor Matthiessen has pointed this out in *The Achievement of T. S. Eliot, op. cit.*, p. 73. Michael Roberts, writing on Eliot's poetry in *The London Mercury*, XXXIV (1936), 39, also shows how Eliot applied his theory: "In his early poems, he followed the method of Henry James or Ezra Pound: the story is told from the point of view of a *persona* and that *persona* (Prufrock or any one of the half-dozen characters of *The Waste Land*) is mistaken by some readers for the author himself. In his later poems, Mr. Eliot has gradually modified this method; the earliest *personae* were characters in whom the poet could see something of his own problems, but from whom he was detached and remote; later, in the Ariel Poems, he came nearer to identifying himself with his characters, but made them remote in time and place from himself. Finally, in his recent work, the choruses for *The Rock* and *Murder in the Cathedral*, he speaks in words which have a meaning for himself, and a different and equally valid meaning for the bricklayers or the charwomen of the chorus."

[39] *Sel. Essays*, p. 51.

the impression of a voice speaking, but not for the purpose of addressing an audience or trying to persuade his readers to accept some view which he is trying to expose. It is rather in the nature of a soliloquy; and if we recall that Eliot said "that a poem, in some sense, has its own life," he would seem to be saying that the object of Hopkins' lyric poetry is mimetic. On the other hand, the speech is suggestive of Hopkins' own speech—the poet is speaking in his own voice. Therefore, in manner, it would be non-mimetic; it would not be an assumed voice or the voice of an imagined character.[40]

As for narrative, in speaking of *Ulysses,* Eliot pointed out that Joyce used the myth as "a way of controlling, or ordering, of giving a shape and a significance" to the immense panorama which was his material. This was the function of the *mythos* in Aristotle and several of Eliot's commentators have pointed out that

---

[40] See *Sel. Essays,* p. 38. Here Eliot described the typical convention about voice in the lyric: "There is in fact no conversational or other form which can be applied indiscriminately; if a writer wishes to give the effect of speech he must positively give the effect of himself talking in his own person or in one of his roles. . . ." On the other hand a passage on Yeats (*The Southern Review,* VII, 449) suggests the dramatic theory very forcefully: "The lyric poet—and Yeats was always lyric, even when dramatic—can speak for every man, or for men very different from himself; but to do this he must for the moment be able to identify himself with every man or other men; and it is only his imaginative power of becoming this that deceives some readers into thinking that he is speaking for and of himself alone—especially when they prefer not to be implicated." But where the Aristotelian theory would detach the voice in the poetic object from the personal speech of the poet, Eliot keeps the poet's voice and would identify his speech with mankind. The Greek theory is simpler and devoid of the implications of the poet speaking as seer. Cf. also an interesting passage by Valéry, *Poésie et Pensée abstraite* (London: Oxford University Press, 1939), pp. 25-26: "Songez aussi qu'entre tous les arts, le nôtre est peut-être celui qui coordonne le plus de parties ou de facteurs indépendants: le son, le sens, le réel et l'imaginaire, la logique, la syntaxe et la double invention du fond et de la forme . . . et tout ceci au moyen de ce moyen essentiellement pratique, perpétuellement altéré, souillé, faisant tous les métiers, le *langage commun,* dont il s'agit pour nous de tirer une Voix pure, idéale, capable de communiquer sans faiblesses, sans effort apparent, sans faute contre l'oreille et sans rompre la sphère instantanée de l'univers poétique, une idée de quelque *moi* merveilleusement supérieur à MOI."

he has done the same thing in his own works.[41] In fact, in "Four Elizabethan Dramatists," there is a description of the object of poetry which is most Aristotelian in substance:

> The imitation of life is circumscribed, and the approaches to ordinary speech and withdrawals from ordinary speech are not without relation and effect upon each other. It is essential that a work of art should be self-consistent, that an artist should consciously or unconsciously draw a circle beyond which he does not trespass: on the one hand actual life is always the material, and on the other hand an abstraction from actual life is a necessary condition to the creation of the work of art.[42]

What art must imitate, of course, is nature or "actual life." Since it may not copy actual life exactly and conform to the conditions of art, a certain abstraction is necessary. But the important thing both in the imitation and in the abstraction is to maintain consistency within the structure formed. This Eliot has always insisted upon. Because the Greeks demanded the *mythos,* there would be less likelihood of too much abstraction—the great danger of modern art; on the other hand, by calling for a conformity to a story, the danger of lack of unity by too great imitation of the details of actuality was averted.

---

[41] *The Dial*, LXXV (1923), 483. In *Scrutinies*, II, Alec Brown tried to show that Eliot was essentially a lyric poet and therefore he distorted his talent by attempting to write in any other than the conventional lyric form. Mr. Brown in his analysis of *The Waste Land* shows a certain obtuseness in understanding that poem. It was as early as 1926 that I. A. Richards pointed out that what Eliot had written was an epic. By using allusion as a technical device, Eliot had been able to compress into 433 lines "the equivalent in content to an epic. Without this device twelve books would have been needed" (*The Principles of Literary Criticism*, N. Y.: Harcourt, Brace & Co., 1926, p. 290). Also Matthiessen has written that Eliot found a "scaffold for his poem" in the Grail legend. By this *mythos* he gained a dramatic shaping for his material. Because Eliot is so conscious of the subjectivism that has seeped into psychology and epistemology since the Renaissance, Matthiessen comments, he felt the necessity of grounding the structure of his longest poem in something outside himself, in an objective pattern of myths.

[42] *Sel. Essays*, p. 111.

When we turn to the third form, however, and Eliot says: "Who is more dramatic than Homer or Dante?" what does he mean by *dramatic?* His explanation follows:

> We are human beings, and in what are we more interested than in human actions and human attitudes? Even when he assaults, and with supreme mastery, the divine mystery, does not Dante engage us in the question of the human attitude towards this mystery—which is dramatic? Shakespeare was a great dramatist and a great poet. But if you isolate poetry from drama completely, have you the right to say that Shakespeare was a greater dramatist than Ibsen, or than Shaw?[43]

A close examination of this text will show that here Eliot is equating dramatic with the object of poetry, the meanings or *genre,* not with the manner of representing it. Aristotle had limited the object to "human actions." Eliot stresses "human attitudes." Since he does not explain what he means by this, it is impossible to say whether he is referring to the inevitable feelings and emotions or not. But in a passage which occurs in *A Garland for John Donne* there is a section which glosses the word *dramatic* very succinctly:

> Donne, Corbière, Laforgue begin with their own feelings and their limitation is that they do not always get much outside or beyond; Shakespeare, one feels, arrives at an objective world by a process from himself, whoever he was, as the centre and starting point; but too often, one thinks with Browning, here is a world with no particular interesting man inside it, no consistent point of view. But the verse method, in all these four men, is similar: either dramatic monologue or dramatic dialogue; and with Donne and the French poets, the pattern is given by what goes on within the mind, rather than by the exterior events which provoke the mental activity and play of thought and feeling.[44]

---

[43] *Ibid.,* p. 51. Francis Birrell in an article entitled "The Poetic Drama Once More," *The Nation and The Athenaeum* (July 7, 1928), 470, points out that Eliot uses *drama* to refer indiscriminately to a stage play and the spectacle of the human soul in action.

[44] *A Garland for John Donne,* p. 14.

Although this passage is interesting for what it says, it is still more arresting for the general position it describes. It reveals Eliot's interest in dramatic method (and in these particular poets, whom he mentions) by citing Donne and the others because they suggest addressees to whom their poems are directed as speeches, but not because Eliot has any conscious theory of lyric as a mimetic structure. Over and above that, it is impressive because of the emphasis upon the subjective in the first part of the quotation, despite the apparent objectivity of method. All of these poets "begin with their own feelings and they . . . do not . . . get much outside or beyond [them]," we are told.[45] The matter of the work then becomes the feelings of the poets. Granting that it is possible for these to become "impersonal," as Eliot describes them and to relate by means of the objective correlative these feelings and the poetic object, would it be possible to say that such poetry is a re-presentation? Aristotle had called the object of the poetic work a *mythos,* and, from the kind of poetry with which he was familiar, had insisted that its presence was necessary for "poetry." Because poetry represented this in words, he classified it ontologically as *imitation.* And in this sense poetry is unique; it exists actually in the real world as a structure of forms, but its form is only mimetic, ontologically speaking. Its words are structuralized by many formal elements; but philosophically speaking, poetry has no substance of its own. It is *imitation.* Therefore, for Aristotle speech that is called poetry is never presented; it is always re-presented. This does not mean that it has to be reportorial. "For art is concerned neither with things that are, or come into being, by necessity, nor with things that do so in accordance with nature (since these have their origins in themselves) and art has its origin in the maker" (*N.E.* 1140a12-15, Ross's tr.). In Eliot's theory both in the manner, that is by the voice, and in the object, that is by the meanings given in poetry, though there are attempts to explain these as objective, both refer eventually to the poet, speaking in his own voice and suggesting affective meanings which are in some manner identified with the poet.

---

[45] Aristotle, of course, commended the description of passions when they were necessary or consonant for the dramatic action; but he ascribed the affections to the characters not to the artist.

Yet, since Eliot professes to be following Aristotle in some respects, does he ever use the word *imitation;* and, if so, does he understand it in this sense?

Speaking of Wordsworth in *The Use of Poetry,* he calls his "new version of Imitation" the "best so far": "Aristotle, I have been told," Eliot quotes Wordsworth, "has said that Poetry is the most philosophic of all writing; it is so; its object is truth, not individual and local, but general, and operative."[46] But what Eliot understands by, or what he thinks Wordsworth means by general and operative truth in poetry he does not explain. In the light of the emphasis upon affectivity, one can only conjecture that he thinks that if the emotional meanings are eventually realized, then poetry conveys truth of an affective sort. But Wordsworth's "I have been told" borders on the foolish; and if he had been a trifle more sceptical and examined for himself, he would have found that the conclusion he drew could not be attributed to Aristotle.[47] There is no such thing as a "general and operative" truth. Truth is a transcendental attribute which can only be postulated of classes of objects in relation to an intellect. Poetry is a generic term which covers a class of objects, each one of which exists and as such is true to itself. If Eliot means that, then he may say that "its object is truth." But this is hardly what he means.[48]

In the few other places where Eliot has used the term *imitation,* he has followed the normative rhetorical tradition,[49] a fact which

---

[46] *Use of Poetry,* p. 75. Cf. Ker's comments upon Wordsworth's position in *Form and Style,* pp. 197-198.

[47] This passage recalls something which Eliot quoted in his review of *The Letters of J. B. Yeats, op. cit.,* p. 90: "The substance of poetry, Mr. Yeats says, is 'truth seen in passion.' To most readers this will fall into memory—for it is an easy phrase to remember—along with something said by Matthew Arnold, or Wordsworth, or Professor Saintsbury; but Mr. Yeats means what he says."

[48] A good discussion of the relation of truth to poetry is contained in Sidney Zink's "Poetry and Truth," *Philosophical Review,* LIV (March, 1945): 132-154.

[49] Though lip service was paid to the term *imitation* among the ancients, it meant largely the copying of literary models—the meaning that had been stressed in the Greek rhetorical schools. The doctrines from these schools

has been alluded to in the conclusion of Professor Wilson's article, "Imitation": "The practice of imitating models has now few advocates; yet it is notable that T. S. Eliot has described a discipline in a normative literary tradition in some ways suggestive thereof."[50] Eliot explains his theory of imitation and its relation to tradition best perhaps in a well-known passage from the essay on "Philip Massinger": ,

> One of the surest of tests is the way in which a poet borrows. Immature poets imitate; mature poets steal; bad poets deface what they take, and good poets make it into something better, or at least, something different. The good poet welds his theft into a whole of feeling which is unique, utterly different from that from which it was torn; the bad poet throws it into something which has no cohesion. A good poet will usually borrow from authors remote in time, or alien in language, or diverse in interest.[51]

Imitation in this sense is not simply a copying; it is a making after a fashion, and it is the fashion which Eliot has used most abundantly in his own work. That it gives him great pleasure to expound this method may be seen from what he says about Ben Jonson: "His third requisite in a poet pleases me especially: 'The third requisite in our poet, or maker, is *Imitation,* to be able to convert the substance, or riches of another poet, to his own use!'"[52] This use of imitation is definitely in the rhetorical tradition and has no connection with re-presentation or imitation as Aristotle used the term. But whether one calls it imitation or stealing, what

---

had in turn influenced the Romans. Poetic was then subsumed under rhetoric by the Sophists and remained in this subordinate position until the Renaissance. Not until the sixteenth century did anything like the metaphysical implications of the term become known. On the other hand, the rhetorical influence of imitation provided a normative discipline in literary criticism until the nineteenth century.

[50] H. S. Wilson, Shipley's *Dictionary,* art. "Imitation," pp. 315-317.

[51] *Sel. Essays,* p. 206. Remy de Gourmont says that only poets "remote in time" are "profitable" to study. *Le Problème,* pp. 24-25. For other texts from Eliot on imitation, see *Sel. Essays,* p. 336; 320-321; and *The Criterion,* VII (1927), 153.

[52] *Use of Poetry,* pp. 54-55.

it is welded into as far as Eliot is concerned is "a whole of feeling."

As Eliot points out in "Experiment in Criticism," Horace dominated literary criticism until the nineteenth century. Though veiled by misconceptions for a long time, it is now rather conclusively settled that the *differentia* of poetry for Horace "was not *imitatio* but *incitatio*."[53] Therefore, the Horatian tradition is in effect the rhetorical tradition. The article, "Poetry and Prose," in Shipley's *Dictionary,* concludes by noting that the conception of poetry in the rhetorical tradition "has never wholly died . . . though it has been assimilated to others and in various ways refined." One of the ways it has been refined may be seen by scrutinizing Eliot's theory. In the essay on John Dryden in *The Use of Poetry* there is a passage quoted from Dryden's "Preface" to the *Annus Mirabilis* which deals with the poet's relation to the poem:

> The first happiness of the poet's imagination is properly invention, or the finding of the thought; the second is fancy, or the variation, deriving, or moulding of that thought, as the judgement represents it proper to the subject; the third is elocution, or the art of clothing and adorning that thought, as found and varied, in apt, significant, and sounding words; the quickness of the imagination is seen in the invention, the fertility in the fancy, and the accuracy in the expression.[54]

There are several interesting and significant developments which arise from Eliot's discussion of this analysis, especially, his stressing that the whole process is purely one of imagination. Historically speaking, the description is engaging because of the use of two of the three terms describing the process. What Aristotle had applied exclusively to rhetoric, "invention" and "elocution," on a purely intellectual level is here linked with fancy and made to describe the poetic process on an almost exclusively perceptual level. But it is the wholehearted acceptance of this as an adequate description

---

[53] For a discussion of this, see J. C. La Drière, *American Journal of Philology,* LX (1939) : 288-300; also Shipley's *Dictionary,* art. "Poetry and Prose," pp. 441-445.

[54] *Use of Poetry,* p. 55.

of his own method of writing that makes the passage significant
for Eliot, for he notes:

> We are liable, I think, to underrate Dryden's critical
> analyses, by assuming that they only apply to the kind
> of poetry that he writes himself. . . . Even if Dryden's
> poetry seems to us of a peculiar, and, as it has seemed
> to many, a peculiarly unpoetic type, we need not con-
> clude that his mind operated quite differently from those
> of poets at other periods.[55]

Now in the rhetorical tradition, since the speech of poetry is
not considered a re-presentation, it must be direct speech or
presentation, and this is exactly what Eliot has called it when he
wrote: "Permanent literature is always a presentation: either a
presentation of thought, or a presentation of feeling by a statement of events in human action or objects in the external world."[56]
Permanent literature includes both poetry and prose. From the
examples which he cites the presentation of thought is ostensibly
"prose." Aristotle "presents thought" and in doing so is also a
great writer. "The *Agamemnon* or *Macbeth* is equally a statement,
but of events." In his explanation Eliot asserts that both of these
types of work are productions of the "intellect." To make either
of them intellectual activity is necessary, or, as Aristotle said, they
involve a "true course of reasoning" (*Nichomachean Ethics,*
1140a10). But in a good example of the second type, such as *Education Sentimentale,* the intellect is engaged "in refraining from
reflection, in putting into the statement enough to make reflection
unnecessary." The work which presents feeling, in other words,
must not be used as a vehicle for abstract thinking on the part of the
poet or be used to present an abstract thought, but must present
such a number of concrete details that whatever effect the writer
wishes to produce can be done without reference to generalities.
All that the poet aims to do is "to set something down."[57]

---

[55] *Ibid.,* pp. 57-58.

[56] *Sac. Wood.,* p. 58.

[57] *Ibid.,* p. 170. For other texts in which Eliot describes poetry as a statement, see *Sel. Essays,* pp. 213, 319, 243; *Sac. Wood,* p. 68; *Collected Poems
of Harold Monro,* p. xv; *The Wheel of Fire,* p. xviii; *Le Serpent,* p. 13;
The Dial, LXXXIII (1927), 259; *The Athenaeum* (May 9, 1919), 298.

Both rhetoric and poetic are for Eliot a presentation. Though he tries to differentiate them upon the basis of thought and feeling, psychologically this is impossible. Any statement that carries reasoned discourse must arouse thought before it evokes emotion. In fact, the emotion is possible only because meanings, which have been derived from the words employed, have first been understood. Dividing these meanings into abstract and concrete references, or presentation of thoughts and presentation of events, would hardly be sufficient *differentiae* since in an example which he gives, Plato's *Theaetetus,* "the particular setting, and the abstruse theory of knowledge afterwards developed, co-operate without confusion."[58] Another exemplification of this fusion of concrete and abstract to which Eliot is constantly referring is Dante's *Purgatorio.* On the other hand, the presentation of thought may not be unaccompanied by emotional response. At any rate, Eliot's conception of poetry as a presentation agrees well enough with the Horatian tradition in which the poetic process is one of communication.

We must next consider the *differentia,* intensity of artistic process, which has been isolated in Eliot's implicit definition. The poem as an object is a structure of words and sounds. By these an objective correlative presents an "emotion in art." Eliot holds that if the poetic object is well made, and objective intensity is discernible, the emotion, which is an objective art emotion and is contained in the object, will be immediately communicated. Though rather dubious about calling the process "communication," nevertheless, he states that "what is communicated is the poem itself."[59] But even an objectified intensity is too closely associated with the theory of expressionism to justify its consideration as an adequate *differentia;* and Eliot has not sufficiently severed the discourse in which this intensity occurs from the rhetorical tradition to secure a complete objectivity for poetry as its own ontological right.

This chapter has been called "The Clarification of the Center." That title can be relevant to Eliot's theory only if it shows that there is really no center to clarify. Eliot has modified the Horatian tradition of presenting a statement by emphasizing that what is

---

[58] *Ibid.,* p. 65.
[59] *Use of Poetry,* p. 30.

important for poetry is not the statement as such but the accompanying affectivity of that statement. This would link his theory to a romantic theory of expression. Eliot has tried to avoid this by placing his *differentia* in the object at such moments as the ensemble of structural elements achieves such artistry that the affective meaning is clearly embodied in the work and an effect which he calls intensity is achieved. By stressing the making of this affectivity into a structure which uses words that refer to "objects, situations, or chains of events" he has introduced an element of the Aristotelian theory of art as the making of an object. So what we have in Eliot's theory is no partisan affiliation to any one tradition but a combination of certain elements of all three of the traditions woven together.

CHAPTER V

THE SACRED WOOD

> Why had I not the wit to avail myself of the sub-
> terfuge, and, like Peter, to renounce my identity,
> especially, as in certain moods of mine, I have often
> more than doubted of it myself? When a man is, as
> it were, his own front-door, and is thus knocked at,
> why may he not assume the right of that sacred wood
> to make every house a castle, by denying himself to
> all visitations?
>
> J. R. Lowell

> It is difficult . . . to make the facts generalize them-
> selves.
>
> T. S. Eliot

This survey of Eliot's criticism, made in an effort to deduce
his *differentia* of poetry, began with a statement that Eliot recognized an "urgent need" for a study of critical terms. An acceptance
of this challenge and an application of it to his use of the term
poetry shows how importunate this need is. Though it has not
been the purpose of this study to evaluate Eliot's theory in relation to that of other critics, still he has acknowledged his indebtedness to others; and there is ample proof that his criticism is as
much a sacred wood as is his poetry. What emerges from his
corpus of writings is not one system but a structure of eclectic
theory. He has established a theoretical concept, but because his
theory is an admixture of elements from three traditions, the various parts do not cohere without violence. There is consistency of
individual doctrines which do not synthesize into a logical whole.

His refusal to emerge from the sacred wood and to label any
metaphysical house as his own results in this structure. Perhaps,
Eliot has done this purposely. He has constantly deprecated his
own critical efforts, and in 1920 he wrote in *The Chapbook* that
"the critic of poetry needs the same professional equipment as the

poet." But, if this study has done nothing else, it has at least pointed to the fact that the critic, if he is to be consistent and clear, must have an explicit philosophical background.

Eliot's survey of verse is important because it shows his recognition of the importance of sound structure in poetry. His polite disregard for the traditional means of studying English prosody shows that he is acutely conscious of the problem facing critics and those interested in these matters. By asserting the impossibility of describing English verse according to traditional systems of prosody, Eliot has pointed to one of the basic reasons for so much inept criticism. We can say nothing pertinent because we have not the tools to find out anything definite. English *is* an amalgam of languages, and the effort to force English rhythms into patterns developed for other languages may account for one phenomenon in the work but leaves many others unexplained. But what Eliot has suggested is equally inept. If poetry uses rhythms in its own right, then any adequate explanation can only be elucidated by a scientific study of *that* use—not by a vague comparison with other types of discourse or with other arts. Then the rhythms of modern English poetry will be understood as the distinct phenomena which they are. If Eliot believes that poetry is a generic form of discourse whose sound structure is equal in importance to its meaning structure, if he believes that poetry should be taken seriously, then it deserves organized investigation to determine some system whereby the rhythms of English poetry may be suitably measured and discussed to obtain definite facts. Though some few efforts have been made, such investigation is still very limited.

Eliot's theory of poetry has been developed from a notion that was fostered by medieval and early Renaissance theorists who held that poetry was a subdivision of rhetoric. Into this he was largely drawn by following the stylistic injunctions of Ezra Pound and the principles of John Dryden. Much that Eliot has to say on the technique of writing is taken from these sources. Though the topics these writers stressed are legitimate discussion for poetry, nevertheless, because such criticism has developed largely under the rhetoricians, and because Eliot has repeatedly refused to make a statement separating poetry from rhetoric, one may justly conclude that poetry for him, as for Dante, is *fictio rhetorica in musica posita.*

In Eliot's work, his championship of Aristotle has resulted in the formulation of many important facts which need stressing in modern criticism. The integration that should exist between the sound and meaning structures is definitely an extension of the Aristotelian principle of unity. Furthermore, Eliot has indicated that the process which he favors is that of making an object. Though his description is overlaid with affective terminology, what is eventually pointed to as being made is a structure of objective correlatives; that is, a structure of references of words to things in the objective world.

The endeavor to separate poetry from other intellectual disciplines by means of final cause is a notable achievement too for modern criticism; and even if at times Eliot himself is a little half-hearted about stressing the emotional function of poetry, as though he would like to champion a more serious and graver purpose, his persevering insistence that "poetry is not a substitute for philosophy or theology or religion" at least points to the fact that, however modest, poetry has a niche of its own, even though Eliot refuses to state what it is.

Besides the lack of a metaphysical center, much of the confusion in Eliot's criticism is owing to a psychological terminology which is not sharp enough. He has not only used the terms *emotions* and *feelings* indiscriminately, but he has also in his efforts to explain metaphysical poetry described one psychological effect in terms of another. What is cognitive must remain so; what is affective, is likewise fixed. One can never become the other. It is true that one of the virtues of modern psychology is the demonstration of that close relation of these things and of the effect one has upon the other; but "thought" can never "become sensation," nor "sensation," "thought."

Though ostensibly renouncing the theory of poetry as a process of expression, especially of expressing personality, he is so insistent upon the affective stimulations to be derived from poetry that one is led to conclude that Eliot conceives poetry as a process of expressing emotion. By the use of the objective correlative and by referring to art emotions, he has tried to erect an "impersonal theory"; but this is vitiated by an inconsistent and vague terminology about emotions and feelings, intensity, and sensibility until one is forced to conclude that, whatever his intentions, Eliot is still tangled in the web of nineteenth-century critical diction. Eliseo Vivas has concluded his study of Eliot by remarking that "the vocabulary of the emotions is . . . confusing, if not indeed irrelevant, to literary criticism." How confusing it is, can only be fully appreciated by one who has endeavored to wrestle honestly with Eliot's facts to make them generalize correctly. If criticism is to emerge from the sacred wood of romanticism into the broad daylight of scientific reality, the first thing that must be done is to assign poetry to its ontological position in the scheme of reality. Without this foundation criticism becomes a floating island in the region of Laputa. In almost every generalization that has been drawn in this study, Eliot has escaped the toils of subjectivism into which his romantic vocabulary would ostensibly ensnare him. But the purity of Aristotle to which he aspired in *The Sacred Wood* has not been attained. The extent of the objectivity which Eliot has achieved will only be fully realized after all of his relations with Dryden, Coleridge, Remy de Gourmont, Ezra Pound, T. E. Hulme, I. A. Richards, G. M. Hopkins, and Paul Valéry have been studied. Eliot has borrowed from all of these but never repetitively. What he has taken has always suffered a sea-change. The miracle of his criticism, encased though it is in a romantic vocabulary and riding in the territory of expressionism, is that it has somehow eluded romantic capture.

SELECTED BIBLIOGRAPHY

I. BIBLIOGRAPHICAL

Eliot, Henry Ware. "T. S. Eliot, [Unpublished] Catalogue of the Collection." Houghton Library, Harvard University.
Fry, Varian. "A Bibliography of the Writings of Thomas Stearns Eliot." *Hound and Horn,* I: 214-218; 320-324.
— Gallup, Donald C. *A Catalogue of English and American First Editions of the Writings of T. S. Eliot.* Portland: Southworth-Antheonsen Press, 1937.
Stallman, Robert. "Selective Bibliography on the Criticism of Poetry, 1920-1942," *The University Review* (Un. of Kansas City), X (Autumn, 1943) : 59-63.

II. PRIMARY TEXTS

1. BOOKS

After Strange Gods. London: Faber & Faber, 1934.
The Classics and the Man of Letters. London: Oxford University Press, 1943.
Essays, Ancient & Modern. London: Faber & Faber, 1936.
Ezra Pound, His Metric and Poetry. New York: A. A. Knopf, 1917.
For Lancelot Andrewes. Garden City: Doubleday, Doran & Co., 1929.
John Dryden, the Poet, the Dramatist, the Critic. N. Y.: Terence & Elsa Holliday, 1932.
The Music of Poetry, Glasgow: Jackson Sons & Co., 1942.
The Sacred Wood. London: Methuen & Co., 1934, 3rd ed.
Selected Essays, 1917-1932. London: Faber & Faber, 1932.
The Use of Poetry and the Use of Criticism. London: Faber & Faber, 1933.
What Is a Classic? London: Faber & Faber, 1945.

2. PREFACES, INTRODUCTIONS, ESSAYS, ETC.

Baudelaire, Charles. *Intimate Journals.* Translated by Christopher Isherwood. N. Y.: Random House, 1930. "Introduction," pp. 7-26.
Dobrée, B. (ed.). "Byron," *From Anne to Victoria.* N. Y.: Charles Scribner's Sons, 1937, pp. 601-619.
Jones, P. M. (ed.). "Johnson's 'London' and 'Vanity,'" *English Critical Essays of the Twentieth Century.* London: Oxford University Press, 1933, pp. 301-310.

Kipling, Rudyard. "Essay," *A Choice of Kipling's Verse.* N. Y.: Charles Scribner's Sons, 1943, pp. 5-36.

Knight, G. Wilson. *The Wheel of Fire.* London: Oxford University Press, 1930. "Introduction," pp. xi-xix.

Monro, Harold. *Collected Poems.* Edited by Alida Monro. London: Cobden-Sanderson, 1933. "Critical note," pp. xiii-xvi.

Moore, Marianne. *Selected Poems.* London: Faber & Faber, 1935. "Introduction," pp. 5-12.

Perse, St. — J. *Anabase.* N. Y.: Brentano's, Inc., 1945. "Preface" [62-65].

Philippe, Charles-Louis. *Bubu of Montparnasse.* Translated by Laurence Vail. Paris: Crosby Continental Editions, 1932. "Preface," pp. vii-xiv.

Pound, Ezra. *Selected Poems.* Edited by T. S. Eliot. London: Faber & Gwyer, 1928. "Introduction," pp. vii-xxv.

Read, Herbert (ed.). "A Note on the Verse of John Milton," *Essays and Studies by the Members of the English Association,* XXI (1936), 32-40.

Ridler, Anne (ed.). *The Little Book of Modern Verse.* London: Faber & Faber, 1941. "Preface," pp. 5-9.

Spencer, Theodore (ed.). "Donne in Our Time," *A Garland for John Donne, 1631-1931.* Cambridge: Harvard University Press, 1931, pp. 1-19.

Tradition and Experiment. "Experiment in Criticism." London: Oxford University Press, 1929, pp. 198-215.

Valéry, Paul. *Le Serpent.* Translated by Mark Wardle. London: R. Cobden-Sanderson, 1924. "A Brief Introduction to the Method of Paul Valéry," pp. 7-15.

Wilson, Edmund (ed.). "In Memory of Henry James," *The Shock of Recognition.* N. Y.: Doubleday, Doran & Co., 1943, pp. 854-865.

Wilson, J. Dover (ed.). "A Note on Two Odes of Cowley," *Seventeenth Century Studies Presented to Sir H. J. C. Grierson.* London: Oxford University Press, 1938, pp. 235-242.

3. PERIODICALS

American Prefaces
  "Literature and the Modern World," I (1935), 19-22.
The Athenaeum
  "Beyle and Balzac" (May 30, 1919), 392-393.
  "Kipling Redivivus" (May 9, 1919), 297-298.
  "The Poetic Drama" (May 14, 1921), 635.
The Bookman
  "Poetry and Propaganda," LXX (1930), 595-602.
The Chapbook
  "A Brief Treatise on the Criticism of Poetry," II (Mar., 1920), 1-10.
  "Prose and Verse," No. 22 (Apr., 1921), 3-10.

The Criterion
> "Dramatis Personae," I (1922-23), 303-306.
> "Commentary," II (1923-24), 371-375.
> "Commentary," III (1924-25), 341-344.
> "Commentary," IV (1926), 627-629.
> "Grammar and Usage," V (Jan., 1927), 121-124.
> "Commentary," VI (1927), 289-291.
> "Mr. Lucas's Webster," VII (1928), 155-158.
> "Commentary," XI (1931-32), 680.
> "Commentary," XII (1932-33), 244-249.
> "Housman on Poetry," XIII (1933-34), 151-154.
> "Commentary," XIV (1934-35), 610-613.
> "Commentary," XV (1935-36), 458-463.
> "Commentary," XVI (1936-37), 63-69.
> "A Review of *Nightwood*," XVI (1936-37), 560-564.
> "Commentary," XVI (1936-37), 666-670.

The Dial
> "Emotional Unity," LXXXIV (1928), 109-112.
> "Isolated Superiority," LXXXIV (1928), 4-7.
> "Literature, Science, and Dogma," LXXXII (Jan.-June, 1927), 239-243.
> "London Letter," LXXII (1922), 510-513.
> "Marianne Moore," LXXV (July-Dec., 1923), 594-597.
> "The Silurist," LXXXIII (1927), 259-263.
> "Ulysses, Order and Myth," LXXV (1923), 480-483.

The Egoist
> "Contemporanea," V (1918), 84-85.
> "Disjecta Membra," V (1918), 55.
> "The Letters of J. B. Yeats," IV (1917), 89-90.
> "Observations," V (1918), 69-70.
> "Professional, or . . ." V (1918), 61.
> "Reflections on Contemporary Poetry," IV (1917), 133-134.

The Listener
> "John Dryden," III (Apr. 16, 1930), 688-689.
> "The Minor Metaphysicals," III (Apr. 9, 1930), 641-642.
> "The Devotional Poets," III (Mar. 26, 1930), 552-553.
> "Rhyme and Reason," III (Mar. 19, 1930), 502-503.
> "Thinking in Verse" (Mar. 12, 1930), 441-442.

The Monist
> "The Development of Leibniz's Monadism," XXVI (1916), 534-556.

The Nation & Athenaeum
> "John Donne" (June 9, 1923), 331-332.
> "The Mysticism of Blake" (1927), 779.

The New English Weekly
> "That Poetry Is Made with Words," XV (Apr. 27, 1939), 27-29.

The New Republic
  "The Idealism of Julien Benda," LVIII (1928), 105-107.
The New Statesman
  "The Borderline of Prose," IX (May 19, 1917), 157-159.
  "Reflections on *Vers Libre,*" IX (Mar. 3, 1917), 517-519.
La Nouvelle Revue Française
  "Note sur Mallarmé et Poe," XXVI (1926), 524-526.
Poetry
  "Ezra Pound," LXVIII (September, 1946), 326-338.
Purpose
  "On a Recent Piece of Criticism," X (Apr.-June, 1938), 90-94.
The Sewanee Review
  "The Man of Letters and the Future of Europe," LIII (1945), 333-342.
The Southern Review
  "The Poetry of Yeats," VII (1941-42), 442-454.

III. GENERAL

1. BOOKS

Aristotle. *The Works of Aristotle.* Edited by W. D. Ross. Vol. XI. Oxford: Clarendon Press, 1924.

Batteux, M. L'Abbé. *Principes de la Littérature.* Tome Premier. Paris: Dessint & Saillant, 1775.

Brown, Alec. "The Lyric Impulse in the Poetry of T. S. Eliot," *Scrutinies,* II. Edited by Edgell Rickword. London: Wishart & Co., 1931.

Bywater, Ingram. *Aristotle on the Art of Poetry.* Oxford: Clarendon Press, 1909.

Cargill, Oscar. *Intellectual America.* N. Y.: Macmillan Co., 1941.

Coffey, Peter. *Ontology.* N. Y.: Peter Smith, 1938.

Croce, Benedetto. *Aesthetics.* Translated by Douglas Ainslie. 2nd ed. London: Macmillan & Co., 1922.

Coleridge, S. T. *Biographia Literaria.* Edited by J. Shawcross. 2 vols. Oxford: Clarendon Press, 1907.

Daiches, David. *New Literary Values.* London: Oliver & Boyd, 1936.

Dolmetsch, Arnold. *The Interpretation of the Music of the XVIIth and XVIIIth Centuries.* N. Y.: H. W. Gray & Co., 1917.

Dryden, John. *Essays.* Edited by W. P. Ker. 2 vols. Oxford: Clarendon Press, 1926.

Guérard, A. *Robert Bridges.* Cambridge: Harvard University Press, 1942.

Gourmont, Remy de. *La Culture des Idées.* Paris: Mercure de France, 1900.
———. *Le Problème du Style.* Paris: Mercure de France, 1924.

Hall, Vernon. *Renaissance Literary Criticism.* N. Y.: Columbia University Press, 1945.

Hartog, Sir Philip. *On the Relation of Poetry to Verse.* English Association Pamphlet, 64. London: Oxford University Press, 1926.

Hayward, John. *Points of View.* London: Faber & Faber, 1941.

Higgins, Bertram. "The Critical Method of T. S. Eliot," *Scrutinies,* II. Edited by Edgell Rickword. London: Wishart & Co., 1931.

Hopkins, Gerard M. *Correspondence,* Vol. II. Edited by C. C. Abbott. London: Oxford University Press, 1935.

Horatius Flaccus, Quintus. *Satires, Epistles and Ars Poetica.* Translated by H. R. Fairclough. Loeb Library Series. N. Y.: G. P. Putnam's Sons, 1926.

Hughes, Glenn. *Imagism and the Imagists.* Stanford, Calif.: Stanford University Press, 1931.

Hulme, T. E. *Speculations.* Edited by Herbert Read. London: K. Paul, Trench, Trubner & Co., 1924.

Issacs, J. "Coleridge's Critical Terminology," *Essays and Studies,* Vol. XXI. Edited by Herbert Read. Oxford: Clarendon Press, 1936, pp. 86-104.

Kazin, Alfred. *On Native Grounds.* N. Y.: Reynal & Hitchcock, 1942.

Ker, W. P. *Form and Style in English Poetry.* Edited by R. W. Chambers. London: Macmillan & Co., 1928.

La Drière, J. C. "Form," "Poetry and Prose," "Voice and Address," "Classification," "Expression," "Prosody," *Dictionary of World Literature.* Edited by J. T. Shipley. N. Y.: The Philosophical Library, 1943.

Matthiessen, F. O. *The Achievement of T. S. Eliot.* N. Y.: Oxford University Press, 1935.

———. *American Renaissance.* N. Y.: Oxford University Press, 1941.

Mercier, D. F. F. J. Cardinal. *A Manual of Scholastic Philosophy.* Translated by T. L. and S. A. Parker. 2 vols. London: K. Paul, Trench, Trubner & Co., 1932.

Nolte, F. O. "Imitation as an Aesthetic Norm." *Art and Reality.* Lancaster, Pa.: Lancaster Press, Inc., 1942.

Oras, Ants. *The Critical Ideas of T. S. Eliot.* Tartu, Estonia: J. C. Krüger, 1932.

Petersen, Julius. *Die Wissenschaft von der Dichtung.* Erster Band: Werk und Dichter. Berlin: Junker und Dünnhaupt Verlag, 1931.

Phillips, R. P. *Modern Thomistic Philosophy.* 2 vols. London: Burns, Oates & Washbourne, 1934.

Pollock, Thomas C. *The Nature of Literature.* Princeton: Princeton University Press, 1942.

Porteus, H. G. *Wyndham Lewis.* London: Desmond Harmsworth, 1932.

———. *The Spirit of Romance.* N. Y.: E. P. Dutton & Co., n. d.

Pound, E. L. *Polite Essays.* Norfolk, Conn.: New Directions, n. d.

Praz, Mario. "Donne and the Poetry of His Time," *A Garland for John Donne, 1631-1931.* Edited by T. Spencer. Cambridge: Harvard University Press, 1931.

Ransom, J. C. *The New Criticism.* Norfork, Conn.: New Directions, 1941.

Richards, I. A. *Principles of Literary Criticism.* 2nd ed. N. Y.: Harcourt, Brace & Co., 1926.

Rickword, Edgell (ed.). *Scrutinies,* II. London: Wishart & Co., 1931.

Shipley, Joseph T. (ed.). *Dictionary of World Literature.* N. Y.: The Philosophical Library, 1943.

Stace, W. T. *The Meaning of Beauty.* London: Grant Richards and Humphrey Toulmin, 1929.

Tate, Allen. *Reason in Madness.* N. Y.: G. P. Putnam's Sons, 1941.

Valéry, Paul. *Poésie et Pensée abstraite.* Oxford: Clarendon Press, 1939.

————. *Les Divers Essais sur Leonard de Vinci.* Paris: La Librairie d'Amateurs, Gilbert Jeune, 1931.

Wilson, H. W. "Imitation," *Dictionary of World Literature.* Edited by J. T. Shipley, N. Y.: The Philosophical Library, 1943.

Winters, Y. *The Anatomy of Nonsense.* Norfolk, Conn.: New Directions, 1943.

————. *Primitivism and Decadence.* Norfolk, Conn.: New Directions, 1939.

2. PERIODICALS

Birrell, Francis. "The Poetic Drama Once More." *The Nation & Athenaeum,* XLIII (July 7, 1928), 470.

Giovannini, G. "Agnolo Segni and a Renaissance Definition of Poetry," *Modern Language Quarterly,* VI (June, 1945), 167-173.

Häusermann, Hans. "T. S. Eliots Religiöse Entwicklung," *Englische Studien,* LXIX (1935), 372-391.

————. "T. S. Eliot's Conception of Poetry," *Etude de Lettres,* Oct. 1, 1942, 165-180.

Hodgson, R. A. "Tradition and Mr. Eliot," *The New English Weekly,* XIX (Sept. 25, 1941), 221-222.

Hopkins, G. M. "Early Poems and Extracts from the *Notebooks* and *Papers* of G. M. Hopkins," *The Criterion,* XV (1935-36), 1-17.

Hulme, T. E. "Notes on Language and Style," *The Criterion,* III (1924-25), 485-497.

La Drière, J. C. "Horace and the Theory of Imitation," *American Journal of Philology,* LX (1939), 288-300.

Loring, M. L. S. "T. S. Eliot on Matthew Arnold," *Sewanee Review,* XLIII (Oct., 1935), 479-488.

Pound, Ezra. "George Antheil," *The Criterion,* II (1923-24), 32-1331.

————. "Vers Libre and Arnold Dolmetsch," *The Egoist,* IV (1917), 90-91.

————. "Arnold Dolmetsch," *The Egoist,* IV (1917), 104-105.

————. "Mr. Eliot's Mare's Nest," *The New English Weekly,* IV (1934), 500.

Praz, Mario. "T. S. Eliot and Dante," *The Southern Review,* II (1937), 525-548.

Rees, Garnet, "French Influence on T. S. Eliot," *Revue de Littérature Comparée,* XVI (1936), 764-767.

Rivière, Jacques. "La Crise du Concept de Littérature," *La Nouvelle Revue Française,* XXII (1924), 159-170.

Roberts, Michael. "The Poetry of T. S. Eliot," *London Mercury,* XXXIV (1936), 38-44.

Schwartz, Delmore. "T. S. Eliot as the International Hero," *The Partisan Review,* XII (1945), 199-206.

———. "Anywhere Out of the World," *The Nation,* CLVII (1943), 102-103.

Vivas, Eliseo. "The Objective Correlative of T. S. Eliot," *The American Bookman,* I (1944), 7-18.

Walsh, Dorothy. "The Cognitive Content of Art," *The Philosophical Review,* LII (1943), 433-451.

Weiss, T. "The Nonsense of Winter's Anatomy," *The Quarterly Review of Literature,* I (1943-44), 212-234; 300-318.

Zink, Sidney. "Poetry and Truth," *The Philosophical Review,* LIV (1945), 132-154.